Local Provision of Public Services: The Tiebout Model after Twenty-Five Years

STUDIES IN URBAN ECONOMICS

Under the Editorship of

Edwin S. Mills
Princeton University

Norman J. Glickman. ECONOMETRIC ANALYSIS OF REGIONAL SYSTEMS: Explorations in Model Building and Policy Analysis

J. Vernon Henderson. ECONOMIC THEORY AND THE CITIES

Norman J. Glickman. THE GROWTH AND MANAGEMENT OF THE JAPANESE URBAN SYSTEM

George S. Tolley, Philip E. Graves, and John L. Gardner, URBAN GROWTH POLICY IN A MARKET ECONOMY

David Segal (Ed.). THE ECONOMICS OF NEIGHBORHOOD

R. D. Norton. CITY LIFE-CYCLES AND AMERICAN URBAN POLICY

John F. McDonald. ECONOMIC ANALYSIS OF AN URBAN HOUSING MARKET

Daniel Feenberg and Edwin S. Mills. MEASURING THE BENEFITS OF WATER POLLUTION ABATEMENT

Michael J. Greenwood. MIGRATION AND ECONOMIC GROWTH IN THE UNITED STATES: National, Regional, and Metropolitan Perspectives

Takahiro Miyao. DYNAMIC ANALYSIS OF THE URBAN ECONOMY

Katharine L. Bradbury, Anthony Downs, and Kenneth A. Small. FUTURES FOR A DECLINING CITY: Simulations for the Cleveland Area

Charles F. Mueller. THE ECONOMICS OF LABOR MIGRATION: A Behavioral Analysis

Douglas B. Diamond, Jr. and George S. Tolley (Eds.). THE ECONOMICS OF URBAN AMENITIES

Alex Anas. RESIDENTIAL LOCATION MARKETS AND URBAN TRANSPORTATION: Economic Theory, Econometrics, and Policy Analysis with Discrete Choice Models

Joseph Friedman and Daniel H. Weinberg. THE ECONOMICS OF HOUSING VOUCHERS

George R. Zodrow (Ed.). LOCAL PROVISION OF PUBLIC SERVICES: The Tiebout Model after Twenty-Five Years

Local Provision of Public Services: The Tiebout Model after Twenty-Five Years

Edited by

George R. Zodrow
Department of Economics
Rice University
Houston, Texas

1983

ACADEMIC PRESS

A Subsidiary of Harcourt Brace Jovanovich, Publishers

New York   London
Paris   San Diego   San Francisco   São Paulo   Sydney   Tokyo   Toronto

ACADEMIC PRESS RAPID MANUSCRIPT REPRODUCTION

*Proceedings of the Peterkin Symposium on Local Provision of Public Services:
The Tiebout Model after Twenty-Five Years
Held April 16 – 17, 1981 at Rice University*

COPYRIGHT © 1983 BY ACADEMIC PRESS, INC.
ALL RIGHTS RESERVED.
NO PART OF THIS PUBLICATION MAY BE REPRODUCED OR
TRANSMITTED IN ANY FORM OR BY ANY MEANS, ELECTRONIC
OR MECHANICAL, INCLUDING PHOTOCOPY, RECORDING, OR ANY
INFORMANTION STORAGE AND RETRIEVAL SYSTEM, WITHOUT
PERMISSION IN WRITING FROM THE PUBLISHER.

ACADEMIC PRESS, INC.
111 Fifth Avenue, New York, New York 10003

United Kingdom Edition published by
ACADEMIC PRESS, INC. (LONDON) LTD.
24/28 Oval Road, London NW1 7DX

Library of Congress Cataloging in Publication Data
Main entry under title:

Local provision of public services: The Tiebout model
  after twenty–five years

  (Studies in urban economics)
  1. Public goods--Addresses, essays, lectures.
2. Municipal services--Addresses, essays, lectures.
3. Local finance--Addresses, essays, lectures.
4. Property tax--Addresses, essays, lectures.
5. Intergovernmental fiscal relations--Addresses,
essays, lectures. I. Zodrow, George R. II. Title:
Tiebout model after twenty–five years. III. Series.
HB864.5.L62 1983   363   83–6405
ISBN 0–12–781820–0

PRINTED IN THE UNITED STATES OF AMERICA

83 84 85 86   9 8 7 6 5 4 3 2 1

Contents

Contributors ix
Preface xi

1. **The Tiebout Model after Twenty-Five Years: An Overview**   1
   George R. Zodrow

   I. Introduction   1
   II. An Overview   2
   III. Conclusion   13
   References   14

2. **The Theory of Local Public Goods Twenty-Five Years after Tiebout: A Perspective**   17
   Joseph E. Stiglitz

   I. Introduction   17
   II. The Fundamental Theorems of Welfare Economics with Local Public Goods   19
   III. Sufficient Conditions for the Efficiency of Local Public Goods Equilibrium   26
   IV. Inefficient Local Public Goods Equilibrium   35
   V. Land Capitalization   41
   VI. Rental Capitalization   45
   VII. Redistribution   45
   VIII. The Decentralization of Pareto Efficient Allocations   47
   IX. Conclusion   50
   References   52

3. **Beyond Tiebout: Modeling the Political Economy of Local Government**   55
   Susan Rose-Ackerman

   I. Introduction   55
   II. The Limits of Tiebout Models: How Far Can One Push the Competitive Analogy?   57

    III. Exit and Voting in Local Government Models 63
    IV. Toward a Political Economy of Local Government 73
        References 78

4. **A Review: Is the Property Tax a Benefit Tax?** 85
    Bruce W. Hamilton

    I. Introduction 85
    II. The Tiebout Orthodoxy 86
    III. Challenges to the Orthodoxy 92
        References 104

5. **The Incidence of the Property Tax: The Benefit View versus the New View** 109
    George R. Zodrow and Peter Mieszkowski

    I. Introduction 109
    II. Zoning, Capitalization and the Allocative Effects of the Property Tax 111
    III. Interjurisdictional Competition and the New View of the Property Tax 118
    IV. General Evaluation and Conclusions 126
        References 128

6. **Income Redistribution in a Federal System** 131
    William H. Oakland

    I. Introduction 131
    II. The Model 133
    III. Optimal Federal Redistribution 136
    IV. Deductibility of Local Taxes 137
    V. Regional Cost of Living or Amenity Differentials 138
    VI. Tax Avoidance or Elastic Labor Supply 140
    VII. Conclusion 143
        References 143

7. **Are Property Taxes Capitalized into House Values?** 145
    Howard S. Bloom, Helen F. Ladd, and John Yinger

    I. Introduction 145
    II. Studies Based on Aggregate Data 149
    III. Studies Based on Cross-Sectional Micro-Data 153
    IV. Studies Based on Micro-Data Representing Tax Changes 157
    V. Conclusions and Suggested Further Research 160
        References 162

8. Voting and Spending: Some Empirical Relationships in the Political Economy of Local Public Finance   165
Thomas Romer and Howard Rosenthal

    I. Introduction   165
   II. Perception and Intergovernmental Aid   168
  III. Budget Cuts and Learning   172
  IV. The Size of Majorities   174
   V. Voter Turnout in Budget Elections   178
  VI. SMSA vs. Other Districts   180
 VII. Conclusion   180
      References   182

Contributors

Numbers in parentheses indicate the pages on which the authors' contributions begin.

Howard S. Bloom (145), Program in City and Regional Planning, John F. Kennedy School of Government, Harvard University, Cambridge, Massachusetts 02138

Bruce W. Hamilton (85), Department of Political Economy, The Johns Hopkins University, Baltimore, Maryland 21218

Helen F. Ladd (145), Program in City and Regional Planning, John F. Kennedy School of Government, Harvard University, Cambridge, Massachusetts 02138

Peter Mieszkowski (109), Department of Economics, Rice University, Houston, Texas 77251

William H. Oakland (131), Department of Economics, Tulane University, New Orleans, Louisiana 70118

Thomas Romer (165), Graduate School of Industrial Administration, Carnegie-Mellon University, Pittsburgh, Pennsylvania 15213

Susan Rose-Ackerman (55), School of Law, Columbia University, New York, New York 10027

Howard Rosenthal (165), Graduate School of Industrial Administration, Carnegie-Mellon University, Pittsburgh, Pennsylvania 15213

Joseph E. Stiglitz (17), Department of Economics, Princeton University, Princeton, New Jersey 08540

John Yinger (145), Program in City and Regional Planning, John F. Kennedy School of Government, Harvard University, Cambridge, Massachusetts 02138

George R. Zodrow (1, 109), Department of Economics, Rice University, Houston, Texas 77251

Preface

The chapters in this volume describe the current state of the art in several theoretical and empirical branches of economic research related to Charles Tiebout's provocative hypothesis that consumer mobility and interjurisdictional competition result in an efficient allocation of resources to the local public sector. This volume is especially topical in light of recent proposals to return responsibility for the provision of many public services to state and local governments. It provides many important insights on the issues currently being considered in policy debates regarding the appropriate means of providing essential public services.

The papers on which this volume is based were presented at the Peterkin Symposium on Local Provision of Public Services: The Tiebout Model after Twenty-Five Years, held at Rice University on April 16–17, 1981. Many people deserve thanks for making the symposium a success. Most importantly, the symposium was made possible by the generosity of George A. Peterkin, Jr., and the Peterkin family, who have contributed greatly over the years toward making the research environment at Rice a stimulating one. The program discussants, David Bradford and Edwin Mills of Princeton University, Dennis Epple of Carnegie-Mellon University, and Robert Stein of Rice University, were primarily responsible for the active exchange of ideas that took place at the conference; many of their perceptive comments are reflected in the final versions of the papers. Gordon Smith was instrumental in organizing the symposium as well as in ensuring that it proceeded smoothly, and Vera Wallis cheerfully handled a wide variety of tasks associated with hosting the conference. The manuscript was typed by Jerry Mays, and Maria Ballivian proofread the volume. Finally, special thanks are due to Peter Mieszkowski, who generously provided assistance and counsel from the initial planning stages of the symposium to the final publication of this conference volume.

Chapter 1

THE TIEBOUT MODEL AFTER TWENTY-FIVE YEARS:
AN OVERVIEW

George R. Zodrow

Department of Economics
Rice University
Houston, Texas

I. INTRODUCTION

Twenty-five years ago, Charles Tiebout responded to Paul Samuelson's (1954) exposition of the theory of pure public goods with his classic article "A Pure Theory of Local Expenditures." In that paper, he set forth what is now known as the "Tiebout model," a model where consumer mobility and competition among local jurisdictions result in an efficient allocation of resources to the local public sector.

Tiebout's result was based on very strong assumptions. On the demand side, he assumed that consumers had perfect information regarding the revenue and expenditure policies of a large number of local jurisdictions and that they were perfectly mobile (consumer income was not affected by choice of residence). On the supply side, he assumed that local public services exhibited no externalities and that, due to congestion, all communities had an optimal size at which the per capita cost of providing a fixed bundle of public services was minimized; each community sought to attain and then maintain its optimal size. The model yielded correspondingly strong results. Local public services were provided efficiently, since consumers revealed their preferences through their choice of residence and interjurisdictional competition assured that local public services were provided at minimum cost. Moreover, since jurisdictions were homogeneous with respect to tastes for public services, all local public choice problems were eliminated.

Tiebout's proposition concerning the efficiency of the local public sector is no doubt one of the most controversial tenets of the state and local public finance literature. The most striking evidence attesting to this fact is the voluminous literature which has addressed the myriad theoretical and empirical questions raised by Tiebout's original contribution.[1] The papers in this volume represent an important contribution to this literature; the authors synthesize and critically evaluate several of the branches of economic research related to the Tiebout model, present new theoretical and empirical results which shed light on many of the critical questions posed in the literature, and identify areas of agreement while clarifying the nature of the issues yet to be resolved. Specifically, the papers, which are summarized briefly below, focus on: (1) the allocative efficiency characteristics of economies with local public goods; (2) the integration of politics and economics in a system of local governments; (3) the role of the property tax as a benefit tax in a Tiebout framework; (4) the incidence of a national system of locally-controlled property taxes; (5) the interaction between federal and state and local income redistribution programs; (6) the empirical evidence on capitalization in house values of interjurisdictional and intrajurisdictional property tax differences; and (7) the empirical evidence on whether local government bureaucracies can manipulate voting agendas to obtain excessive expenditures on local public services.

II. AN OVERVIEW

A. *The Theory of Local Public Goods and the Tiebout Model*

Tiebout's contribution is frequently viewed as a resolution, at the local level, of the public goods problem posed by Samuelson (1954); in the Tiebout model, consumer mobility and interjurisdictional competition result in an efficient allocation of resources to the public sector. In his contribution, Joseph Stiglitz examines the theoretical basis for this contention.

Stiglitz focuses on the question of whether the two Fundamental Theorems of Welfare Economics can be extended to economies with local public goods (goods which provide no benefits to non-residents of a community but which are public

---

[1]*See Pestieau (1980) for a comprehensive survey of the theoretical and empirical literature related to the Tiebout model.*

goods within the community). That is, he investigates: (1) whether a local public goods competitive equilibrium (if it exists) is Pareto efficient, with an optimal number of communities, an optimal allocation of individuals among communities, and an optimal level of expenditures on public goods within each community; and (2) whether every Pareto efficient allocation in an economy with local public goods can be decentralized. In addressing this question, he stresses the need to specify clearly the information available to the government, the instruments available to the government, the nature of congestion in consumption of the public good or in production, the way that the supply of public goods is determined, the nature of the political process, and the nature of interjurisdictional competition.

Stiglitz constructs two situations, both characterized by a sufficiently large number of communities and perfectly mobile individuals, where the local public goods competitive equilibrium is indeed a constrained Pareto optimum. In the first, there is an infinite number of individuals of each type and complete unanimity regarding public services and taxes even in communities that are heterogeneous with respect to individual tastes and skills. In the second, communities choose public service levels, financed by land taxes, to maximize land rents. In this case, the supply of public goods is efficient, given the allocation of individuals among communities; with an infinite number of identical communities and a large number of identical individuals, the equilibrium is efficient.

However, Stiglitz argues that, for at least five reasons, there is a strong presumption that a local public goods competitive equilibrium will not be Pareto efficient: (1) there are frequently multiple Nash equilibria, some of which are Pareto inferior to others; (2) Pareto optimality may require subsidies between communities which are unlikely to occur; (3) land capitalization may cause landowners to vote for public service packages desired by potential residents rather than current residents; (4) rental capitalization may cause renters to vote for public service packages that are undesirable to potential migrants rather than those desired by current residents; and (5) exclusionary activities by rich communities may result in a population distribution which is not a constrained Pareto optimum. Moreover, arguing along similar grounds, Stiglitz shows that not every Pareto efficient allocation can be decentralized.

Thus, Stiglitz concludes that, except under very stringent conditions, the two Fundamental Theorems of Welfare Economics do not extend to economies with local public goods. However, he notes that decentralized mechanisms for providing public goods have many virtues (*e.g.*, greater responsiveness to local variability, more opportunities for political participation and choice) which, in addition to their allocative efficiency characteristics, must be considered in evaluating the advantages and disadvantages of local provision of public services.

B. *The Integration of Politics and Economics in Local Government*

One essential feature of the Tiebout model is that it eliminates the local public choice problem since the residents of a community are homogeneous with respect to tastes for public services. In her survey of research integrating political and economic aspects of local provision of public services, Susan Rose-Ackerman concludes that "the economist's dream of doing away with politics cannot be realized even in the local government context."

Rose-Ackerman argues that the assumptions made to ensure efficient allocations in Tiebout models are highly unrealistic. Heterogeneous communities, and thus political disagreements, are likely to occur for at least three reasons: (1) people may choose to live in heterogeneous communities to take advantage of scale economies in the production of local public goods; (2) entry of communities is costly so the number of local jurisdictions is limited; and (3) since the supply of housing is relatively inelastic (as is the supply of new communities), differences in public services and taxes will be capitalized in house values and this phenomenon may distort voting patterns.

Rose-Ackerman identifies three types of local government models which consider political choice explicitly. First, she considers majority rule models where voters do not own property. In these models, even when voters' tastes and opportunity sets are defined to ensure a determinate majority rule outcome for any single election, she shows that with migration (which changes the political composition of communities and the opportunity sets facing voters), existence of equilibrium is not assured and, even if existence can be proved, the equilibrium may be neither stable nor efficient.

Second, Rose-Ackerman discusses models where voters are property owners and thus concerned not only with consuming public services and paying taxes but also with the effects of the local fiscal package on house values. Tractable models with capitalization of differences in public services and taxes in house values are difficult to construct because voters must predict the effects of migration on house values and because voters' preferences may not be single-peaked if they are concerned about both capital gains and the local services-tax package *per se*. Research in this area suggests that a Tiebout world is likely to be inefficient due to distortions in the housing market caused by the property tax.[2]

Third, Rose-Ackerman considers monopoly models of local government where a single group or individual makes the political choices in each jurisdiction. Results obtained with these models suggest that under some circumstances, Tiebout-type competition is insufficient to eliminate the "profits" of local government officials, while under other circumstances, the maximization of aggregate property values results in efficient supplies of housing and public services (although the allocation of individuals among communities is not necessarily efficient).

Rose-Ackerman concludes that existing research on the integration of politics and economics in local government has two major failings. From a normative viewpoint, the models neglect the equity implications of the relative immobility of the central city poor and of income segregation in the provision of critical public services like education (the equity problems are even more severe if the production of public services is affected by the demographic characteristics of the population). From a positive viewpoint, there is need for more general models of: (1) the capitalization effects of public choices; (2) the political decision making process in local jurisdictions; (3) the bargaining power of various groups in a multi-government system; and (4) the constraints on local behavior implied by the existence of state and national governments.

C. *The Incorporation of the Property Tax in the Tiebout Framework*

Although Tiebout had little to say about the financing of local public services, his model clearly requires a benefit tax where each individual pays the average (equal to marginal) cost of providing local services. Bruce Hamilton reviews the literature addressing the question of whether the property tax, which provides the bulk of local tax revenues, can be viewed as a benefit tax in a Tiebout framework.

Hamilton addresses both the demand and supply components of this question. On the demand side, he notes that an efficient allocation will result only if consumers face the correct prices; this occurs only if fiscal differentials are perfectly capitalized in house values (for all houses, the sum of house value and taxes equals the sum of the resource cost of providing housing and the average and marginal cost

---

[2] *See Yinger (forthcoming).*

of providing public services). Since perfect capitalization can occur only under fairly restrictive conditions (e.g., a perfectly functioning system of bribes from developers to the local treasury, zoning laws with compensation, total land value maximization by the local government), there is no theoretical presumption that the outcome is efficient. However, since empirical work finds roughly perfect capitalization, Hamilton suggests that, to a good approximation, consumers face the correct prices for local public services; note this implies that no income redistribution occurs through the local fisc.

On the supply side, Hamilton argues that the empirical evidence which finds roughly perfect capitalization suggests that local governments are providing the services demanded; for example, if excessive local services were provided in a jurisdiction, homes there would sell at a discount. Moreover, he notes that there is some presumption that local services are provided efficiently, since inefficient production methods would result in reduced property values.

Hamilton then responds to several of the challenges which have been posed to the Tiebout view of local government. Four of his points are: (1) the scale economies and congestion which lead to the non-constant returns in the production of local public services stressed by Stiglitz and Rose-Ackerman are of little empirical significance; (2) although externalities between communities would result in inefficient allocations, they are also of little empirical significance; (3) the Leviathan monopoly power models, which suggest that local government officials provide excessive (or inefficiently or wastefully produced) public services, assume far too little political acumen on the part of voters and ignore the importance of interjurisdictional mobility as a check on local officials; and (4) the empirical evidence offered by the proponents of Leviathan models in support of their position is unconvincing.

However, Hamilton notes that lower average efficiency in the local public sector is quite probable since neither the detection of inefficiency nor the replacement of an inefficient government by one which will actually be more efficient is likely. He cites empirical evidence of technical regress of 1.5 percent per year in the aggregate state and local public sector to support this contention.[3,4]

[3] *See Hulten (1980).*
[4] *Hamilton also notes income segregation may create equity problems and inefficiencies in both private production (see McGuire, 1974) and public production (see Oates, 1981). Also the Tiebout shopping mechanism complicates individual location decisions (see Hamilton, forthcoming).*

Hamilton concludes that the Tiebout mechanism is fairly effective in ensuring that consumers face correct prices and that supplies equal demands at average cost prices in the local public sector. However, the system is ineffective in ensuring technical efficiency, so that "our system of local government is a price system without efficiency." Since there is little income redistribution through the local fisc, he suggests that increased reliance on private provision of many services currently provided by the local public sector is warranted.

D. *The Tiebout Model and the Incidence of the Property Tax*

Hamilton's work illustrates how the residential property tax can be viewed as a benefit tax within the context of a Tiebout-type model; related research has shown that the non-residential property tax can be viewed as a benefit tax paid by firms for public services received or as compensation to local residents for production externalities.[5] This "benefit view" is in marked constrast to what is known as the "new view" of the incidence of the property tax, a perspective based on the Harberger[6] general equilibrium model of tax incidence, which suggests that capital owners in general bear the burden of a national system of local property taxes.[7] In their contribution, George Zodrow and Peter Mieszkowski examine the different theoretical approaches which lead to such conflicting results regarding the allocative and distributive effects of the property tax.

Zodrow and Mieszkowski focus on two critical differences between the two approaches. First, they note the importance of zoning (or perfect capitalization) in obtaining the benefit view results. Mobility and interjurisdictional competition, in combination with the appropriate residential and non-residential zoning ordinances, ensure that households and firms locate in jurisdictions where tax payments equal public services demanded--or production externalities generated--at the margin. (As noted by Hamilton, perfect capitalization achieves the same result in models without zoning restrictions which result in homogeneous housing.) Thus, the distortionary effect of property taxation on capital allocation across jurisdictions, which is one of the critical elements in the derivation of the new view, is eliminated. To illustrate this point, they show that the benefit view result regarding the incidence of the residential property tax can

---

[5] *See Fischel (1975) and White (1975).*
[6] *See Harberger (1962).*
[7] *See Thomson (1965), Mieszkowski (1972) and Aaron (1975).*

be obtained in a Harberger-type model (which otherwise generates the new view result) simply by imposing the appropriate zoning constraint on housing consumption.

Second, Zodrow and Mieszkowski consider the implications of the Tiebout-type interjurisdictional competition stressed by proponents of the benefit view but ignored in the derivation of the new view. The new view implies that the property tax is a non-benefit tax on capital; they inquire whether such exploitation of capital owners can occur once interjurisdictional competition is taken into account. Their approach is to construct a Cournot-Nash model of interjurisdictional competition where each government sets its property tax rate to maximize the welfare of its residents assuming that all other jurisdictions hold their tax rates fixed; capital is assumed to receive no benefits from local public services. In this case, as long as each government has a head tax at its disposal, the optimal tax rate on mobile capital is zero; the competitive equilibrium is not characterized by non-benefit taxation of capital. However, if each government, for statutory, political or other reasons, can finance local public services only through a property tax on mobile capital, the new view result obtains even in a perfectly competitive environment; also, since each government believes the property tax will drive mobile capital out of its jurisdiction, there is a tendency for local governments to provide an inefficiently low level of public services. However, this constrained Nash equilibrium is unstable in the sense that each community can increase the welfare of its residents by reducing its property tax rate and imposing a head tax.

Zodrow and Mieszkowski conclude that the new view is a viable alternative to the benefit view of the effects of the property tax; that is, the new view of the property tax has relevance even in a world characterized by interjurisdictional competition, as long as the competition does not extend to the use of head taxes rather than property taxes to finance local public services. Under these circumstances, the property tax has a non-benefit component so that allocative efficiency is impaired and, since this non-benefit component is borne by the owners of capital, the property tax is progressive in comparison to a benefit tax.

E. *Interactions Between Local and National Income Redistribution Programs*

The Tiebout model and most of the research related to it has focused on the efficiency aspects of local provision of public services. However, William Oakland argues that a significant amount of income redistribution occurs at the sub-national level since the capitalization mechanism described by Hamilton is imperfect and sub-national governmental units engage in direct redistribution through welfare programs, food stamps, etc. The latter fact suggests that the hypothesis that sub-national governments cannot engage in redistribution[8] assigns an exaggerated role to consumer mobility, especially between urban regions. In contrast, Oakland considers the interaction between local and national redistributive programs in a world of complete consumer immobility.

Oakland constructs a model with two types of individuals (rich and poor) where communities differ only in the fraction of their population which is poor. Both local and national governments choose demogrants and tax rates to maximize the same additive welfare function.[9] The disposable incomes of rich and poor are assumed to be normal goods for each community, so that richer communities have higher disposable incomes for both types of individuals.

Oakland derives four major results: (1) without any explicit or implicit link between local and federal redistributive activity, the standard prescription of federal monopolization of the redistributive function is optimal; (2) if local tax payments are deductible from an individual's federal taxes, some local redistribution will occur since it is effectively being subsidized by the federal government; (3) if amenities (or costs of living) differ among communities, local governments will desire different amounts of redistribution and thus will supplement federal redistributive activity (e.g., if amenities and income are complements, all communities below a cut-off level of amenities will engage in redistribution); and (4) if individuals can avoid taxes or alter their labor supply, the federal government will reduce its redistributive activity, but each local government will augment federal redistribution because it ignores the external effects of its actions on federal tax revenues--too much redistribution may result.

Oakland concludes that sub-national governments are likely to engage in redistributive activity and that the extent of redistribution will vary across communities. While federal redistribution reduces the overall disparities between rich and poor in the nation, it will worsen the plight of the poor in relatively rich communities which finance a disproportionate share of federal redistributive

---

[8] See Oates (1972).

[9] To avoid 100% local tax rates, Oakland assumes that the utility of the rich is weighted more than that of the poor; he shows this is similar to assuming that tax-avoiding opportunities are greater for the rich.

activity. Finally, as demonstrated in the cases when local taxes are deductible from the federal tax base, when amenities or living costs differ among communities, and when individuals are able to avoid taxes or to reduce their labor supply, the redistributive activities of local governments can frustrate federal attempts to achieve a first-best distribution of income even though both levels of government act to maximize the same social welfare function.

F. Empirical Evidence on Capitalization

The papers by Stiglitz, Rose-Ackerman, Hamilton, and Zodrow and Mieszkowski all note the importance of capitalization in the theory of local public finance. In a comprehensive survey of the empirical literature on the capitalization of interjurisdictional and intrajurisdictional property tax differences in house values, Howard Bloom, Helen Ladd, and John Yinger conclude that the literature "presents a cumulative body of evidence indicating a substantial degree of property tax capitalization."

Bloom, Ladd, and Yinger note that although the theory of capitalization is straightforward, empirical estimation of the extent of capitalization is extremely difficult due to: (1) problems of simultaneity bias; (2) problems with left-out variable bias; and (3) problems in determining the appropriate discount rate. Their review focuses on the effects of differences in property taxes, holding public services constant, and considers three branches of empirical research on capitalization.

First, they consider aggregate studies which relate interjurisdictional variations in average house values to variations in average property taxes, controlling for other determinants of house values. In addition to the three problems noted above, these studies suffer from problems in specifying the tax variable (since the effect on house value of a change in the tax rate in a jurisdiction depends on the value of the house) and in measuring differences in public service levels across jurisdictions. The aggregate studies suggest 40 to 90 percent capitalization.

Second, Bloom, Ladd, and Yinger consider both interjurisdictional and intrajurisdictional studies based on cross-sectional data on individual house sales. Since these studies are based on large samples with many housing characteristics, left-out variable bias is not a serious problem; also, tax payments can be measured accurately with micro data, and, for the intrajurisdictional studies, controlling for variation in public service levels is less difficult. Most of the estimates of both interjurisdictional and intrajurisdictional capitalization in this group of studies fall within the 40 to 90 percent range cited above.[10]

Third, they discuss four studies (three intrajurisdictional and one interjurisdictional) which are based on micro data relating changes in individual house values to specific changes in property taxes. In particular, they note that the discount rate is an estimated parameter in their own study;[11] in all of the other studies, the discount rate must be assumed and the estimates of capitalization are very sensitive to its value. All of the studies find consistent evidence of capitalization of changes in the property tax structure; the "best estimate" of capitalization in their study is 90 percent.

Bloom, Ladd and Yinger conclude that the empirical evidence, while not yet conclusive due to methodological problems, is strongly suggestive of substantial interjurisdictional and intrajurisdictional capitalization of differences in property taxes in house values. They suggest that research into the determinants of the extent to which capitalization occurs as well as the theoretical and practical implications of capitalization should be encouraged.

G. *Agenda Setter Models of Local Government Bureaucracy*

As noted by Rose-Ackerman, one set of models which considers both political and economic elements of local government explores the possibility that budget-maximizing local bureaucrats exert monopoly power to expand public services beyond the level desired by the median voter. Thomas Romer and Howard Rosenthal review briefly their theoretical work on one variant of this literature--the *agenda setter model*--and then offer a wide variety of empirical results to support the model.

Romer and Rosenthal describe an agenda setter model where a budget-maximizing bureaucrat confronts the local electorate with a choice between a proposed budget and a reversion budget. Their major theoretical results are: (1) in a world of perfect certainty and perfect information regarding voter preferences and behavior, expenditures exceed the level desired by the median voter except in the case where the reversion level equals the median ideal point (*i.e.*, voters

[10]They show that the only study which does not support the capitalization hypothesis (Wales and Weins, 1974) "is subject to methodological problems that make interpretation of its findings extremely difficult."

[11]See Bloom, Ladd and Yinger (forthcoming).

elect to spend more to avoid low reversion budgets); and (2) with uncertainty regarding voter turnout, the results are theoretically ambiguous, but reversions play an important role in determining expenditure levels.

Romer and Rosenthal then report a wide variety of empirical results based on Oregon school budget elections in support of the agenda setter model (as opposed to the median voter model) of local government expenditure determination. Their major results (and interpretations) are: (1) voters appear to have complete fiscal illusion about state aid but none about local county aid (agenda setters could inform voters about state aid but do not, hoping thereby to increase the size of the local budget); (2) when proposed budgets are defeated and another proposal is submitted to the electorate, the new budget is usually less than, sometimes equal to, but almost never greater than the defeated budget (with uncertainty regarding turnout and a fixed number of elections each year, the optimal budget-maximizing strategy is a sequence of diminishing proposals); (3) there is a negative relationship between the size of the Yes vote on a defeated initial proposal and the magnitude of the difference between the initial and final proposal (with uncertainty regarding voter turnout and preferences, agenda setters "learn" about voter preferences and reduce the size of the proposed budget as little as possible); (4) large majorities seldom occur in school elections in all but the relatively small districts (with certainty and a reversion below the median ideal point, the median voter model implies majorities should be distinctly greater than 50 percent);[12] (5) voter turnout declines with district size (the median voter outcome is less likely and the budget-maximizing outcome is more likely in large districts); and (6) the estimated expenditure equation based on the agenda setter model is not a poorer predictor in metropolitan areas than it is in more isolated areas (as it should be if the increased consumer mobility in metropolitan areas constrains the power of the agenda setter).

Romer and Rosenthal conclude that their empirical evidence argues for continued research on the importance of bureaucratic agenda setting in local government. They suggest that one fruitful area of study is the dynamic adjustments which occur at the local level, which they conjecture are likely to be discontinuous adjustments (e.g., local tax revolts) rather than smooth adjustments around a stable median voter ideal point.

[12]*Romer and Rosenthal also argue that this result cannot be explained within a median voter context even if there is uncertainty about voter preferences.*

III. CONCLUSION

As stressed by Tiebout, local public expenditures comprise a significant fraction of total public services in the United States; for example, total local expenditures (after intergovernmental grants) equaled 64 percent of total federal non-defense expenditures in 1980.[13] Moreover, the local public sector is likely to grow in the near future if a variety of Reagan Administration proposals grouped under the "New Federalism" banner are adopted. Accordingly, an understanding of the economic effects of local provision of public services is essential.

The papers in this volume represent an important contribution to such an understanding. In particular, they focus on Tiebout's contention that consumer mobility and interjurisdictional competition result in an efficient allocation of resources to the local public sector. On balance, the verdict on the narrowly defined efficiency question is rather negative. Local provision of public services can be expected to be efficient only under rather special circumstances, while inefficient outcomes are likely to occur under a wide variety of plausible scenarios as outlined above.

However, from a broader perspective, local provision of public services must be compared to the available alternatives. In those cases where local public services are publicly provided private goods, a strong case can be made for private market provision. Efficiency is quite likely to be improved, as the discipline of the market place is almost certainly more effective in inducing efficient supply than the discipline imposed by the combination of interjurisdictional mobility and the local political process. Moreover, the theoretical and empirical research on capitalization suggests that little redistribution occurs through the local fisc, so that the substitution of private for public provision of these services would have relatively minor equity consequences; this argument loses strength to the extent that the burden of the national system of local property taxes is borne by capital owners.

The cases where local services exhibit the characteristics of public goods are more difficult to evaluate. Although local provision is likely to be inefficient, centralized provision at the federal, state or metropolitan level is also inefficient; empirical estimates suggest that

---

[13]See *Advisory Commission on Intergovernmental Relations (1981). Total state and local government expenditures, after intergovernmental transfers, were slightly greater than total federal non-defense expenditures in 1980.*

the efficiency loss due to centralized provision of uniform service levels is quite large.[14] Moreover, if the federal tax system is viewed as more equitable than local tax systems, the optimal prescription may be federal financing of locally provided public services, so that most of the problems described above would remain.

Thus, local provision of many public services in the United States must be evaluated in light of the available alternatives, rather than according to the Tiebout ideal. The standard criteria of efficiency and equity must be considered, as well as administrative ease, governmental accountability and responsiveness, and the social benefits of greater diversity in public service offerings and more opportunities for citizen participation in the political process. Perhaps the most important contribution of the papers in this volume is a careful delineation of the many problematical aspects of local provision of public services which must be considered when choosing between private and federal, state or local government provision of essential services.

REFERENCES

Aaron, H. J., 1975. *Who Pays the Property Tax?* Washington, D.C.: Brookings Institution.

Advisory Commission on Intergovernmental Relations, 1981. *Significant Features of Fiscal Federalism*. Washington, D.C.: U. S. Government Printing Office.

Bloom, H. S., H. F. Ladd, and J. Yinger, forthcoming. *Property Taxes and House Values*. New York: Academic Press.

Bradford, D. F., and W. E. Oates, 1974. "Suburban Exploitation of Central Cities and Governmental Structure," in H. M. Hochman and G. E. Peterson (eds.), *Redistribution Through Public Choice*. New York: Columbia University Press.

Fischel, W. A., 1975. "Fiscal and Environmental Considerations in the Location of Firms in Suburban Communities," in E. S. Mills and W. E. Oates (eds.), *Fiscal Zoning and Land Use Controls*. Lexington, Mass.: Lexington Books.

Hamilton, B. W., 1975. "Zoning and Property Taxation in a System of Local Governments," *Urban Studies* 12:205-211.

Hamilton, B. W., 1976. "Capitalization of Intrajurisdictional Differences in Local Tax Prices," *American Economic Review* 66:743-753.

Hamilton, B. W., forthcoming. "Wasteful Commuting," *Journal of Political Economy*.

[14]*See Bradford and Oates (1974).*

Harberger, A. C., 1962. "The Incidence of the Corporate Income Tax," *Journal of Political Economy* 70:215-240.

Hulten, C. R., 1980. "A Method of Estimating Public Sector Productivity Change," Urban Institute Working Paper.

McGuire, M. C., 1974. "Group Segregation and Optimal Jurisdictions," *Journal of Political Economy* 82:112-132.

Mieszkowski, P. M., 1972. "The Property Tax: An Excise Tax or a Profits Tax?", *Journal of Public Economics* 1:73-96.

Oates, W. E., 1972. *Fiscal Federalism*. New York: Harcourt, Brace, Jovanovich.

Oates, W. E., 1981. "On Local Finance and the Tiebout Model," *American Economic Review 71 (Papers and Proceedings)*:93-98.

Pestieau, P., 1980. "Fiscal Mobility and Local Public Goods: A Survey of the Empirical and Theoretical Studies of the Tiebout Model," Université Catholique de Louvain, Louvain-la-Neuve, Belgium, Research Program: Spatial Analysis and Public Services Policy, Paper No. 6.

Samuelson, P. A., 1954. "The Pure Theory of Public Expenditures," *Review of Economics and Statistics* 36:387-389.

Thomson, P., 1965. "The Property Tax and the Rate of Interest," in G. C. S. Benson, S. Benson, H. McClelland, and P. Thomson, *The American Property Tax*. Claremont, Cal.: The Lincoln School of Public Finance.

Tiebout, C. M., 1956. "A Pure Theory of Local Expenditures," *Journal of Political Economy* 64:416-424.

Wales, T. J., and E. G. Weins, 1974. "Capitalization of Residential Property Taxes: An Empirical Study," *Review of Economics and Statistics* 56:329-333.

White, M. J., 1975. "Firm Location in a Zoned Metropolitan Area," in E.S. Mills and W.E. Oates (eds.), *Fiscal Zoning and Land Use Controls*. Lexington, Mass.: Lexington Books.

Yinger, J., forthcoming. "Capitalization and the Theory of Local Public Finance," *Journal of Political Economy*.

Chapter 2

THE THEORY OF LOCAL PUBLIC GOODS TWENTY-FIVE YEARS
AFTER TIEBOUT: A PERSPECTIVE[1]

Joseph E. Stiglitz

Department of Economics
Princeton University
Princeton, New Jersey

I. INTRODUCTION

It has long been recognized that there are three fundamental problems associated with the provision of public goods:

(1) *The revelation problem.* For private goods, individuals reveal their preferences in the process of purchasing goods; for public goods, preferences must be elicited in some other way. If individuals' payments for public goods (e.g., taxes) depend on their declared preferences, they will have an incentive to misrepresent their preferences.

(2) *The social choice problem.* Arrow established that there does not exist, in general, a social choice mechanism satisfying the commonly accepted desiderata of (a) non-dictatorship; (b) transitivity; (c) independence of irrelevant alternatives; and (d) Pareto optimality.

(3) *The management of the public good problem.* While for private goods there are strong incentives for firms to provide the goods which individuals wish to purchase and to produce them efficiently, the incentives for citizens to obtain information to select good public managers, and the incentive for public managers to provide for the public good, are either absent or far from perfect.

---

[1]*Financial support from the National Science Foundation is gratefully acknowledged. The author is indebted to Peter Mieszkowski, Robin Lindsey, and David Pearce for their helpful comments.*

Twenty-five years ago, Tiebout (1956) argued that if individuals were mobile among communities, all three problems could be resolved for locally provided public goods, since individuals reveal their preferences by their choice of communities. Communities either provide the goods which individuals wish--and do so efficiently--or individuals leave to other communities that provide public goods which are more in accord with their tastes and which provide these goods more efficiently. Competition among communities is thus like competition among firms for customers, and, just as the latter leads to efficient resource allocations, so too does the former.

In the past twenty-five years a considerable body of literature has been devoted to assessing the validity of Tiebout's contention, both to generalizing Tiebout's model and ascertaining its theoretical limitations, and to testing it empirically.

The objective of this paper is not to present a systematic survey of this voluminous literature.[2] Rather, I would like to return to the fundamental question posed by Tiebout a quarter of a century ago: What implications does the ability of individuals to choose a community have for the provision of public goods? Although there is clearly some similarity between competition among firms in the supply of private goods, is the analogy sufficiently close that the conclusion concerning Pareto optimality established for the former is also valid for the latter?

In the twenty-five years since Tiebout's original contribution, not only have we gained considerable understanding of the questions with which Tiebout was concerned, but we have also learned much about the conditions under which private markets attain a Pareto efficient outcome. For instance, we know that the market allocation is in general not Pareto optimal if (a) there are incomplete futures or risk markets; (b) there is imperfect information, and individuals can acquire information or if one individual's beliefs are affected by the actions of other individuals; or (c) there are non-convexities in production which result in only a subset of the set of potential goods actually being produced.

The basic conclusion of this paper--that it is only under very special and unreasonable assumptions that the process of individual choice among communities leads to Pareto optimality--thus should come as no surprise. Yet I shall argue

---

[2]*For a recent survey, see Pestieau (1980). For another recent treatment of the subject, see Atkinson and Stiglitz (1980), Chapter 17.*

that Tiebout's insight into the importance of choice in the political process is an extremely important one, with numerous policy implications.

II. THE FUNDAMENTAL THEOREMS OF WELFARE ECONOMICS WITH LOCAL PUBLIC GOODS

The central results of modern welfare economics, generally referred to as the Fundamental Theorems of Welfare Economics, establish conditions under which every competitive equilibrium is Pareto efficient, and under which every Pareto efficient allocation can be supported by a competitive equilibrium (with the appropriate lump sum redistributions).

Among the conditions which are conventionally imposed is that there are no public goods. In general, with *pure* public goods the market allocation will not be Pareto efficient. While Pareto efficiency requires that the sum of the marginal rates of substitution equal the marginal rate of transformation, in market equilibrium each individual will equate his own marginal rate of substitution with the price ratio (which equals the marginal rate of transformation in competitive equilibrium).

I am concerned here, however, with a class of public goods which I shall refer to as *local* public goods, the benefits of which accrue only to those who belong to a particular group (which I shall call the community), and not to those who belong to other groups (communities) within the society. There is thus an element of "privateness" in local public goods; while *within* the community the good is a pure public good, *between* communities it is like a private good. Those outside the community receive no benefit. The concept is a natural one; the local public libary in Princeton provides no benefits to the citizens of Houston, and conversely. The question with which I shall be concerned here is under what conditions will the Fundamental Theorems of Welfare Economics be valid for economies with local public goods.

At the outset, I should remark that the analysis presented here reflects only one of the two major strands which have evolved out of the work of Tiebout. In the analysis here, we shall assume that individuals can belong to only one community; they live, work, and play within their own community, and it supplies them with their public and private goods. In the other strand, individuals can belong to many groups; they may live in one community, work in another, and belong to a swimming club which provides one local public good, and to a tennis club which provides another. It is my conjecture that many of the results reported here also apply to this other environment, but a full treatment of this more general case is beyond the scope of this paper.[3,4]

Introducing local public goods requires a reexamination both of what is meant by Pareto efficiency, and what is meant by competitive (market) equilibrium. Both of these turn out to be complicated questions.

A. The Notion of Pareto Efficiency

The basic definition of Pareto efficiency--that no one can be made better off without making someone else worse off --remains, of course, unchanged. However, recent research in welfare economics has emphasized the importance in defining and characterizing the set of Pareto efficient allocations of specifying clearly the information which is available (or more generally, the technology by which information may be acquired), and of defining the set of admissible instruments (e.g., whether lump sum taxes can be employed to redistribute income, whether there are restrictions on the set of risk markets, etc.).[5]

Let me illustrate this point by means of a simple example. We have two groups in the population, those who like public goods and those who do not. There is a single private good (P), and all individuals have identical endowments of a good (I), which can be transformed either into a unit of the public good (G) or of the private good. There are four cases to consider:

[3] Thus, there is some suggestion that the communities implicit in our analysis are more like metropolitan regions than like suburban villages.

[4] It should be emphasized, however, that our analysis of local public goods, like Samuelson's (1954) analysis of pure public goods, is concerned with polar cases; just as there are few pure public goods, there are probably few pure local public goods. It is, however, only by analyzing these polar cases that one can understand the underlying structure of the problems posed by public goods.

[5] Some of these restrictions should, of course, be derived from more fundamental characteristics of the economy. Thus, the restrictions on the ability to employ differential lump sum taxes may be derived from restrictions on the information available to the government which affect its ability to differentiate among individuals; restrictions on the set of risk markets may be derived either from assumptions concerning the transactions costs technology or informational assumptions.

(1) There is perfect knowledge concerning who is a high demander and who is a low demander, and the government can restrict migration. Then Pareto efficiency entails a single community. The set of Pareto efficient allocations are those analyzed by Samuelson (1954), where the *sum* of the marginal rates of substitution equals the marginal rate of transformation. Point A in Figure 1a represents the particular Pareto optimal allocation where a uniform wealth tax is imposed.

(2) There is perfect knowledge concerning who is a high demander and who is a low demander, but migration cannot be restricted. By migrating, individuals can avoid paying any taxes imposed by a community on its residents.[6] Then the set of Pareto efficient allocations which can be supported is restricted. Thus, point A in Figure 1b, which is Pareto efficient with a uniform lump sum tax and no migration, is not an equilibrium. Pareto efficiency will require, in this case, discriminatory taxation (*e.g.*, low demanders are at point B, high demanders are at point C). Without discriminatory taxation, all individuals are at point D.

(3) There is imperfect knowledge concerning who is a high demander, *or* discriminatory lump sum taxation is not allowed, *and* consumption (use) of the public good cannot be monitored. Migration cannot be restricted. Then, the only feasible tax (in this example) is a uniform lump sum tax. Pareto optimality may entail two communities (points X and Y in Figure 1c); but if there is a single community, Pareto optimality will not, in general, entail the sum of the marginal rates of substitution equaling the marginal rate of transformation (point D in Figure 1b).

(4) Under the same assumptions as (3), if now use of the public good can be monitored, Pareto optimality may entail the use of a benefit tax, with a single community rather than two. The gain from the consolidation of the two communities into one exceeds the loss from the distortion associated with the benefit tax (low demanders consume less of the public good than is available (point H in Figure 1c) even though there is zero marginal cost associated with their utilizing more of the public good).[7] Thus, contrary to the popular view, which holds that benefit taxes for public goods are inefficient since they restrict the consumption of something for which the marginal cost of consumption is zero, we show

---

[6]*If lump sum taxes can be imposed independent of residency, then the set of Pareto efficient allocations is the same as in (1) above.*
[7]*Thus, points F and H in Figure 1c satisfy the self-selection constraints; the low demanders prefer H to F although high demanders prefer F to H.*

that, under these quite plausible conditions concerning the information available to the government, benefit taxes may be necessary for Pareto efficiency.

This example illustrates the critical role, in the analysis of Pareto optimal allocations, of assumptions concerning the ability of the government to control migration (to restrict the establishment of new communities), and to discriminate among different citizens, either directly or indirectly (e.g., through benefit taxes).

A third characteristic of the economy that will play an important role in our subsequent exposition concerns *congestion*. In the example just discussed, there is no congestion in the use of the public good, no diminishing returns to scale of the kind that would result from increased transport costs in larger communities, and no diminishing returns in

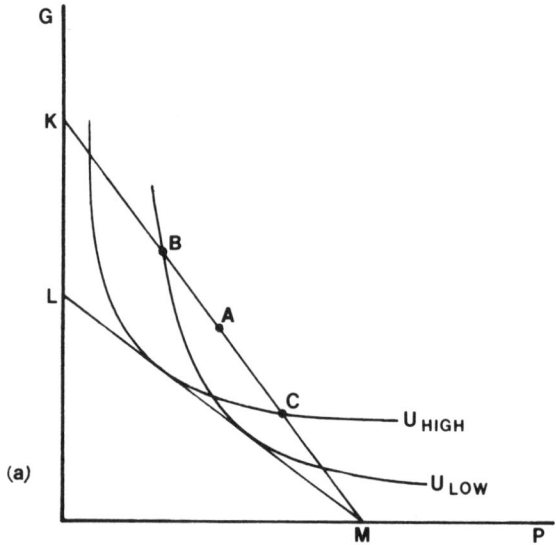

FIGURE 1. *Pareto optimal allocations: (a) Perfect knowledge and no migration. Budget constraint of separate community is LM; budget constraint of merged community is KM (with migration, feasible allocations are BC). (b) Perfect knowledge and migration. With discriminatory lump sum tax, low demanders are at B and high demanders are at C; without discriminatory lump sum tax, all individuals are at D (with no migration and uniform lump sum tax, all individuals are at A). (c) Imperfect knowledge and migration. Without discriminatory taxation, there are two communities at X, Y; a discriminatory non-linear use tax generates a Pareto improvement as there is one community with low demanders at H and high demanders at F.*

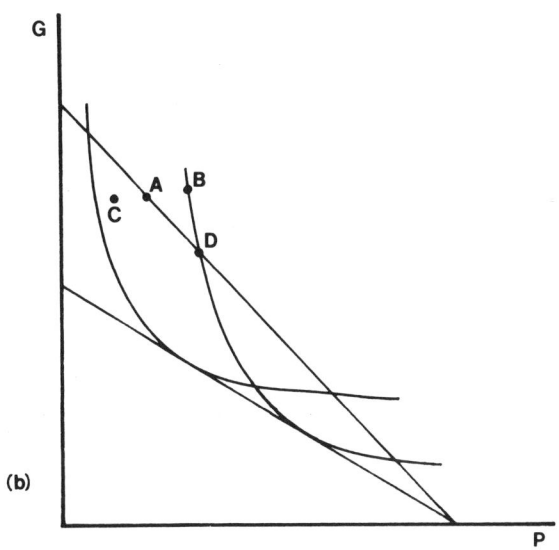

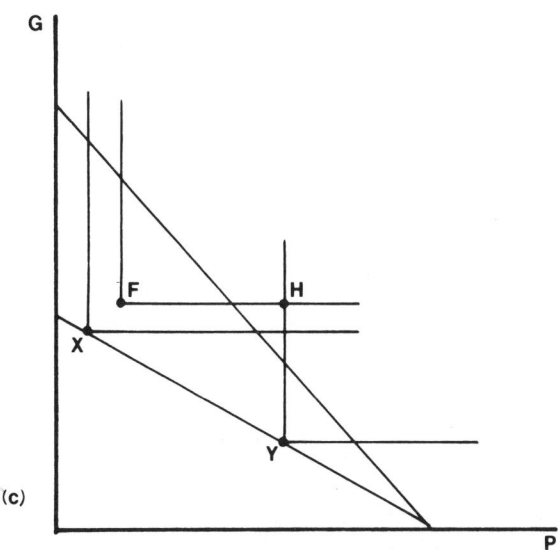

FIGURE 1b,c.

production that would result from increasing the number of workers in a community with, say, fixed land size. That is why when there is perfect information concerning individuals and when discriminatory taxes can be imposed, Pareto efficiency always entails there being a single community. If the congestion effects are strong enough, then even under the above conditions it may be desirable to have more than one community.

For any particular set of assumptions, *e.g.*, concerning migration and the feasibility of discriminatory taxation, we can characterize the set of (constrained) Pareto efficient allocations. In evaluating whether a local public goods equilibrium (to be defined shortly) is Pareto efficient, we shall be particularly concerned with three questions: (a) whether the number of communities is correct; (b) whether the allocation of individuals among communities is correct; and (c) whether the level of expenditures on various public goods within a community is correct.

B. *The Nature of Competitive Equilibrium with Local Public Goods*

The characterization of the local public goods equilibrium also requires us to specify clearly our assumptions concerning migration, the feasibility of discriminatory taxation, and the importance of congestion. In addition, we need to specify how the supply of public goods is determined, the nature of the political process, and the possibilities for "public entrepreneurship."

The "spirit" of the Tiebout conjecture is most appropriately captured, I think, by the free mobility assumption; although certain types of discrimination may be admissible, it is not permissible to discriminate between "original" inhabitants and migrants.

In the subsequent discussion, we shall employ two classes of models. In one, all resources are mobile. Each individual has an endowment of a vector of resources which he can trade with other individuals. A "community" is then a collection of individuals who share in common a set of public goods. The individuals within the community interact in production. The "rules" of the community specify the relationship between the individual's endowments and his consumption of private goods.

In the second, there is one immobile resource, which we can think of as land. The different communities can be thought of as different islands. The critical distinction is then that when an individual moves from one community to another, he does not take his land. (He may still be able to enjoy some return to his land, if the rules of his original community allow those who contribute just land to the community to obtain a return.)

The free migration assumption imposes the requirement that, in equilibrium, individuals of a given type enjoy the same utility in all communities which they inhabit, and the rules of the communities which they do not inhabit, combined with the supply of public goods which these communities provide, generate a level of utility which is less than (or equal to) that level.

If we take as exogenous the number of communities and the rules relating the levels of public goods expenditures and taxes to the number of individuals inhabiting the community, then the only question addressed in the analysis of equilibrium is that of the allocation of individuals among these communities. But one of the primary reasons for interest in the Tiebout mechanism is that individuals' choices convey information about their preferences and--so it is conjectured --this in turn leads to an efficient determination of the level of public goods.

Thus, a complete analysis of the equilibrium requires a specification of the process by which the levels of public goods and taxes are determined. In various parts of this paper we take several alternative approaches:

(1) When there is unanimity on what course of action the government should take, then it is reasonable to assume that the action undertaken is that action which is unanimously favored. The central theorem of Section III.A establishes, in fact, a general condition under which there will be unanimity (even with communities with citizens of different tastes). On the other hand, in the special examples we investigate in Section IV.A, all individuals within a community are identical, and so unanimity is trivial. (The determination of the level of public goods may still not be trivial; what individuals vote for will depend on their perceptions of the consequences--either in terms of migration or land values--of alternative tax-expenditure programs.)

(2) When there are differences in view on what course of action the government should take, we shall assume the level of public goods reflects the preferences of the median voter.[8]

---

[8]*We ignore the problems associated with preferences not being single-peaked, as they often are in the kinds of situations being considered here (see Kramer, 1973; Stiglitz, 1974a; Slutsky, 1977). We employ the median voter model because of its analytical simplicity, making no judgment about the appropriateness of the model as a description of the determination of public goods at the local level.*

The concept of *competition* which is relevant for the analysis of local public goods equilibrium is not obvious. Three assumptions will be employed in the subsequent analysis:

(1) Utility-Taking Communities. Each community faces (or believes it faces) a perfectly horizontal schedule of individuals of each type. Each community is, in other words, a utility taker. This is the natural extension of wage-taking or price-taking behavior for economies in which there are only private goods.

(2) Free Entry. Any entrepreneur can propose a new community, with a new set of rules.

(3) Monopolistically Competitive Communities. Just as there is a widespread view that, when there are fixed costs of producing different commodities, a monopolistically competitive model may be more appropriate than a "perfectly" competitive model, so too here. Although there are many towns (firms), no town (product) is a perfect substitute for any other. There may be systematic biases in the number and variety of towns in the local public goods equilibrium, just as there are biases in the number of firms and the variety of goods they produce in the private goods equilibrium (see Dixit and Stiglitz, 1977; Stiglitz, forthcoming-c; Spence, 1976; Salop, 1979; Lancaster, 1975).

III. SUFFICIENT CONDITIONS FOR THE EFFICIENCY OF LOCAL PUBLIC GOODS EQUILIBRIUM

In the previous section, we attempted to clarify what might be meant both by a Pareto efficient allocation and by a local public goods competitive equilibrium. There has been, since Tiebout's original paper, a widespread belief that a local public goods equilibrium will in fact be Pareto efficient, and that every Pareto allocation with local public goods can be supported by a local public goods competitive equilibrium. This, unfortuately, is not the case, and a major concern of this paper is to explain the primary reasons why this is so.

First, however, it may be useful to begin with two situations where the local public goods competitive equilibrium is a constrained Pareto optimum. The central feature of both situations is that there is a sufficiently large number of communities and that the decision makers in each community take the level of utility of each type of individual as given; if the community offers a utility level below what a particular type of individual can obtain elsewhere, indivi-

The Theory of Local Public Goods

duals of this type will all leave the community, and if they offer a utility level in excess of what the type can obtain elsewhere, there is a flood of immigration.

A. Unanimity in the Provision of Public Goods[9]

We first show that with an infinite number of people of each type, and a sufficiently large number of islands,[10] the local public goods equilibrium (if it exists) is Pareto optimal. Moreover, when each type of individual takes the utility level of other groups as given, there will be complete unanimity both about the level of expenditures on various public goods and the taxes by which those public goods are financed. This is so even though, in general, communities will not be homogeneous, so long as there are productive interactions among individuals or so long as there are transport costs, and different individuals face different transport costs or have different utility functions for land. The focus on homogeneity in so much of the literature is simply a red herring.

To see this, we construct the utility possibilities frontier of the economy. This specifies the maximum amount of utility that can be attained by one type of individual, given the level of utility of other individuals. Because of the free migration assumption, all individuals of a given type attain the same level of utility. (In the absence of public goods, we could have drawn a "factor price frontier" specifying the maximum level of factor price we could pay to one factor, given the factor price paid to the other; as the relative factor price increases, the relative factor intensity decreases. Here the return to participating in a community includes not only the wage, but also the benefits of the public good.)[11]

To see how the utility possibilities schedule can be constructed, we focus, for simplicity, on the case where there are only two groups in the population. Let N_i be the number of individuals of type i in the community and $n = N_1/N_2$. Then for each value of N_1 and N_2 there will be a utility pos-

---

[9]*The results discussed in this section are described in greater detail in Stiglitz (forthcoming-b) and Atkinson and Stiglitz (1980).*

[10]*Identical results obtain if all factors are mobile (i.e., there is no land) so long as there is an infinite number of people of each type.*

[11]*The analogy to "utility-equivalent contracts" discussed in the sharecropping literature (Stiglitz, 1974b) or the labor market literature (Stiglitz, 1975) should be immediate.*

sibilities schedule as depicted in Figure 2a. Next, we construct the fixed-n utility possibilities schedule, where we allow the *number* of individuals on the island to vary as we vary the levels of utility of say U_1. (This utility possibilities schedule may be constructed as the outer envelope of a set of utility possibilities schedules, each of which takes n and, say, $N_1 + N_2$, as fixed; see Figure 2b). Next, we construct the variable-n utility possibilities schedule, as the outer envelope of all of the fixed-n utility possibilities schedules. Figures 2c and 2d illustrate two possible cases.

In Figure 2c, the utility possibilities schedule (for each n) is concave.[12] The outer envelope, giving the utility possibilities schedule for the economy, may or may not be concave. Along the outer envelope, as we increase U_1/U_2, we decrease n. We have thus constructed what is, in effect, a market demand curve for type 1 labor (relative to type 2). The market equilibrium is simply the intersection of this "demand curve" with the curve giving the relative supply (Figure 3a).

In Figure 2d, the utility possibilities schedule (for each n) is convex. Clearly, the outer envelope will then be convex. As we have drawn it, the outer envelope (over a region at least) consists of a small n ($n = n_1$) curve and a large n ($n = n_2$) curve. These dominate intermediate values of n. Thus, for relative supplies of the two types of labor between n_1 and n_2, the levels of utility will be fixed at U_1^* and U_2^*; in equilibrium there will be two types of communities (one with $n = n_1$, and one with $n = n_2$). Changes in the ratio of the aggregate supplies of the two types will be reflected in the mix of the two communities (Figure 3b).

To see that the point we have depicted is in fact the equilibrium, observe that the best any single group could do, given the utility they must offer others to join (or remain in) the community, is to have that resource allocation corresponding to the point on the utility possibilities schedule we have identified as the equilibrium. Moreover, since all groups would thus choose the same point, there is unanimity (even though underlying preferences may differ markedly). Finally, when all communities act in this way, the demands for the different kinds of labor in each community add up precisely to the supply.

Note too that *there is no scope for redistribution within this environment*. Any community attempting to redistribute income against some group will find itself without any of that group in its population.

---

[12]*Even with concave utility functions, the utility possibilities schedule with fixed population may be convex (see Stiglitz, forthcoming-b).*

The Theory of Local Public Goods

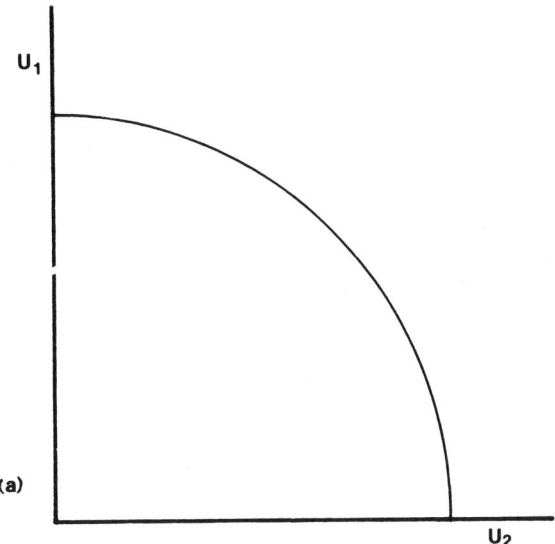

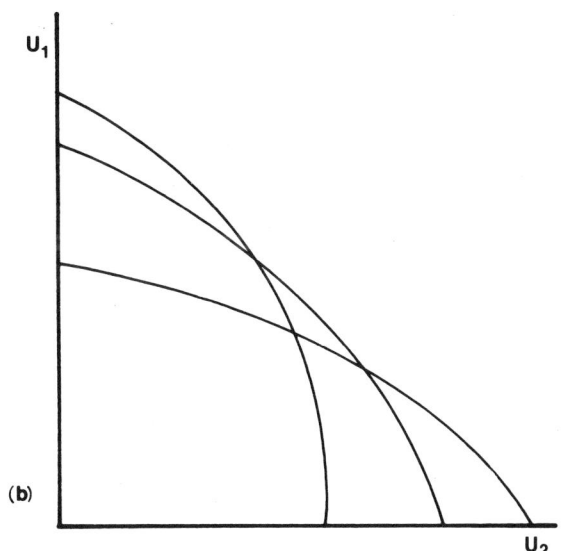

FIGURE 2. Utility possibilities schedules: (a) For fixed island size. (b) For fixed n and island size. Constructed as outer envelope of utility possibilities schedules with same n but different scale. (c) For variable n and island size. Constructed as outer envelope of fixed n utility possibilities schedules. (d) For variable n and island size. Changes in relative supplies of the two types of individuals leave utility levels unchanged (all intermediate values of n are dominated).

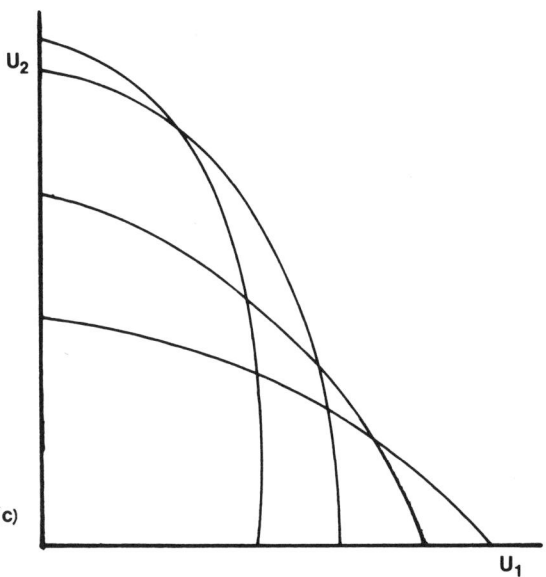

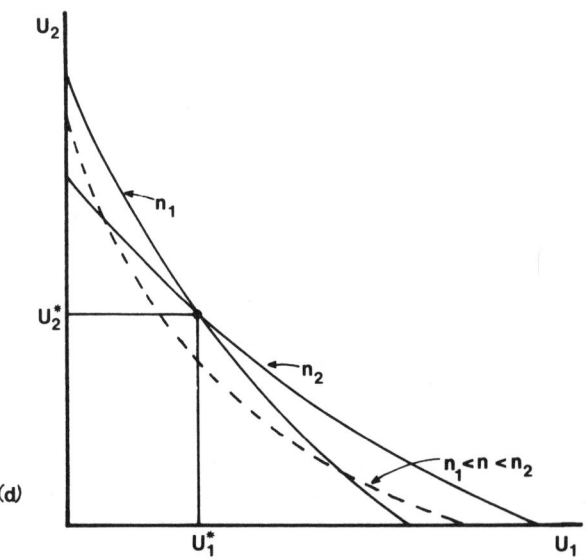

FIGURE 2c,d.

The Theory of Local Public Goods

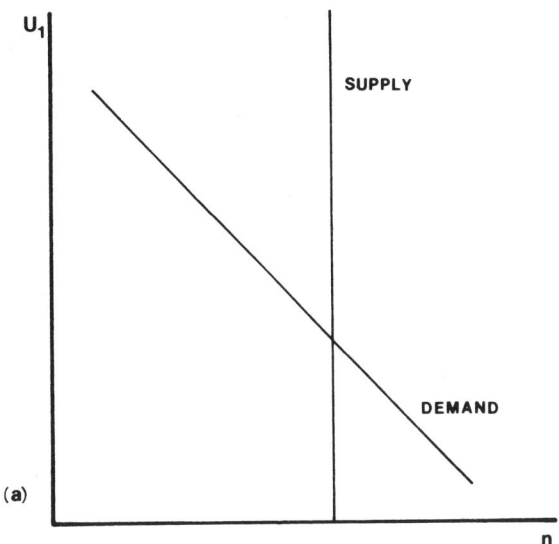

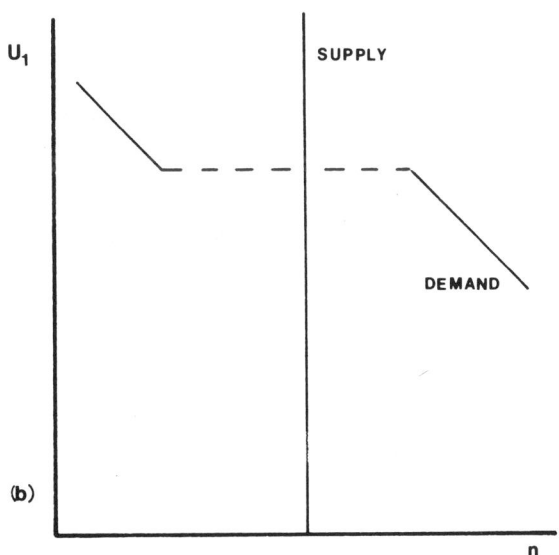

FIGURE 3. Equilibrium as the intersection of demand and supply of labor of type 1: (a) With one type of community. (b) With two types of communities. Changes in relative supplies of different types of labor change the mix of communities.

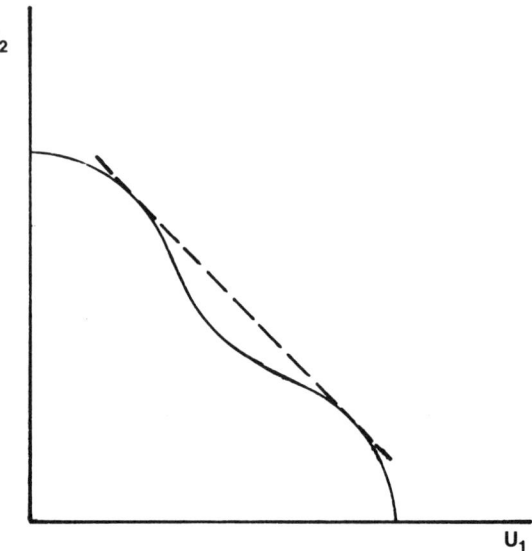

FIGURE 4. *Convex utility possibilities schedule. Randomization improves* ex ante *expected utility of risk-averse individuals.*

Finally, we note that it is possible to show that even with well-behaved concave preferences and technology, the utility possibilities schedule is not concave, as illustrated in Figure 4. If the equilibrium described earlier lies at a point within the convex portion of the utility possibilities schedule, the *ex ante* expected utility clearly can be increased by having two sets of communities, and randomly assigning individuals to one or the other.[13]

B. Land Value Maximization

The second set of conditions under which the local public goods competitive equilibrium is efficient in its supply of public goods entails communities which choose the level of public goods to maximize the value of land rents. Communities which provide more attractive public services will find that individuals are willing to pay higher land rents to live in the community. If each community is a utility taker (in

[13]*Under certain conditions, not only does social optimality (in the sense of maximizing* ex ante *expected utility) entail randomization, but so too will the market equilibrium (see Stiglitz, 1982).*

The Theory of Local Public Goods

the sense defined earlier) and finances the public goods through a land tax, then the level of rent which the ith individual is willing to pay, r^i, is defined implicitly by the modified indirect utility function

$$U^i(Y^i, G, r^i) = \overline{U}^i, \tag{1}$$

where $\overline{U}^i$ is the level of utility obtainable elsewhere, G is the level of public goods, and Y^i is his endowment of income.[14] Total land rents are

$$R = \sum_i r^i T^i, \tag{2}$$

where T^i is the quantity of land consumed by the ith individual. Implicit differentiation of (1) yields

$$-\frac{\partial r^i}{\partial G} = \frac{\partial U^i/\partial G}{\partial U^i/\partial r^i}. \tag{3}$$

But by Roy's formula,

$$T^i = -\frac{\partial U^i/\partial r^i}{\partial U^i/\partial Y^i}. \tag{4}$$

Thus

$$\frac{\partial r^i}{\partial G} = \frac{\partial U^i/\partial G}{\partial U^i/\partial Y^i}\frac{1}{T^i}. \tag{5}$$

This specifies how much additional rent payments individuals are willing to make in response to an increase in the supply of a public good.

The community seeks to maximize net rents $(R - G)$, where, for simplicity, we have assumed that the public good is produced at constant costs, and we have chosen our units so that one unit of the private good can be transformed into one unit of the public good.

Thus, differentiating, $\Sigma \ r^i T^i - G$ with respect to G (holding utility constant), we obtain

[14]*Clearly, we could make the individual's income (e.g., his wage) also depend on the community in which he lives; it should be apparent that this will not alter the analysis.*

$$\sum_i r^i(\partial T^i/\partial G)\big|_U + \sum_i T^i(\partial r^i/\partial G)\big|_U - 1 = 0. \tag{6}$$

In equilibrium the total demand for land must be equal to the total supply, which is fixed; i.e.,

$$\sum_i T_i = \overline{T}. \tag{7}$$

Hence, if in competitive equilibrium $r^i = r$ for all individuals (all individuals face the same prices), then

$$\sum_i r^i(\partial T^i/\partial G)\big|_U = r\sum_i (\partial T^i/\partial G)\big|_U = 0. \tag{8}$$

Substituting (5) and (8) into (6), we obtain

$$\sum_i \frac{\partial U^i/\partial G^i}{\partial U^i/\partial Y^i} = 1. \tag{9}$$

Note that (9) is the familiar Samuelson condition for determining the Pareto efficient supply of public goods: the sum of the marginal rates of substitution must be equal to the marginal rate of transformation (here unity).

We have been careful to assert that land value maximization leads, under the stipulated conditions, to an efficient level of supply of public goods; the equilibrium may still not be Pareto efficient, because the allocation of individuals among communities may be inefficient, as our analysis below will confirm.

There is, however, one set of further restrictions which ensure that the equilibrium is in fact Pareto efficient. Assume that there are an infinite number of identical islands and a very large number of identical individuals. Then there is a Pareto efficient allocation in which public goods expenditure equals land rents in each community and all communities are of identical size.[15,16] This Pareto efficient allocation can be supported by a local public goods competitive equilibrium.

[15]There must be sufficient "congestion" so that it is desirable to have more than one community; see below.

[16]This has been referred to as the "Henry George Theorem" (see Stiglitz, 1977; Arnott and Stiglitz, 1979; Flatters, Henderson, and Mieszkowski, 1974).

IV. INEFFICIENT LOCAL PUBLIC GOODS EQUILIBRIUM

Our earlier analysis identified three important conditions for a local public goods equilibrium to be Pareto efficient: (a) there must be the right number of communities; (b) individuals must be allocated correctly among the communities; and (c) within each community there must be the right supply of public goods.

We shall now see why, under quite plausible conditions, the local public goods equilibrium may be inefficient in all three respects. There are (at least) five problems encountered in ensuring the efficiency of the local public goods equilibrium:

(1) There are often multiple Nash equilibria, some of which are Pareto inferior to others. These inefficiencies are of two types: (a) A homogeneous population is distributed incorrectly among a set of communities; or (b) There is a heterogeneous population, which is grouped into communities (or matched with different islands) inefficiently.

(2) Pareto optimality requires subsidies from one island to another; it is not in the interests of any single community to offer these subsidies.

(3) Because of land capitalization, landowners in each community are more concerned with providing public goods which are attractive to those who are on the margin of moving into their community than they are with the welfare of intra-marginal individuals in their community.

(4) Because of rent capitalization (the fact that rental rates reflect the level of community services offered) renters in each community are more concerned with providing public goods which are relatively *unattractive* to the marginal immigrant than they are with the direct benefits accruing to themselves.

(5) Attempts on the part of rich communities to avoid redistributions to poor migrants not only lead communities to engage in indirect (and often costly) exclusionary activities (which may still be consistent with constrained Pareto optimality), but result in a population distribution which may well not be a constrained Pareto optimum.

A. *Homogeneous Population: Inefficiency in the Number of Communities and the Allocation of Individuals among Communities*

There is a widespread feeling in many countries that the populations of the central cities are too large. The central city, because of its size, can provide many public goods, and it is these public goods which make it so attractive. It is not in the interests of any single individual to migrate to some provincial town; but if enough individuals migrated, the town would be able to provide a high level of public goods. The reduction in crowding in the central city would make such a change a Pareto improvement. A number of governments have, on the basis of some such argument, implemented policies to encourage greater decentralization. The central part of the argument is that the initial situation may, in fact, be a Nash equilibrium, but that there exists another equilibrium which is Pareto superior.

In Figure 5a, we have drawn the maximized value of the utility of the representative consumer in a community as a function of the number of individuals within the community, which we denote by $V(N)$.[17] Very small communities provide a very low level of welfare because they cannot provide much of a supply of public goods; very large communities provide a low level of utility because of crowding (strict concavity of the production function). In the figure, we have depicted the total population, $N = N_1 + N_2$, as exceeding N^*, the optimal population, but being less than twice N^*. Pareto optimality requires that there be two communities. Yet, there is an equilibrium in which only one community is inhabited, provided $V(N) > V(0)$.

Figure 5b illustrates a case where there are multiple Nash equilibria, all except one of which are inefficient. In Figure 5c, we depict a situation where the population is equal to twice N^*. There is still an equilibrium in which there is only one community.

B. Inefficient Matching Nash Equilibria

The problem here is similar to that in the preceding section: there are inefficient allocations of individuals among islands, but no single individual has any incentive to move. There are two islands, one with a long beach but no hills, the other with a beautiful hill for skiing but no beach. There are two types of individuals, skiers and swimmers. For the beach to be usable on the first island requires an expenditure of resources (e.g., constructing an access road); with a much greater expenditure of resources,

[17] *If output (Q) is a function of the number of individuals in the community, $Q = F(N)$, and if the output can be used as either public goods, G, or private goods, then $V(N) = \max U(c,G)$, subject to $F(N) = cN + G$, where c is per capita consumption, and where $U(c,G)$ is the representative individual's utility function.*

The Theory of Local Public Goods

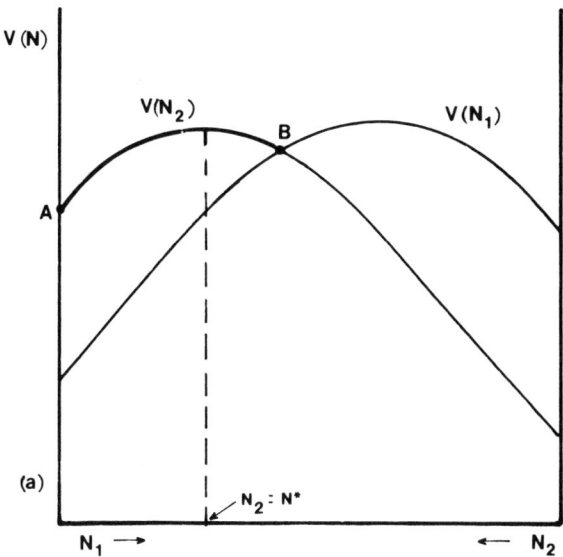

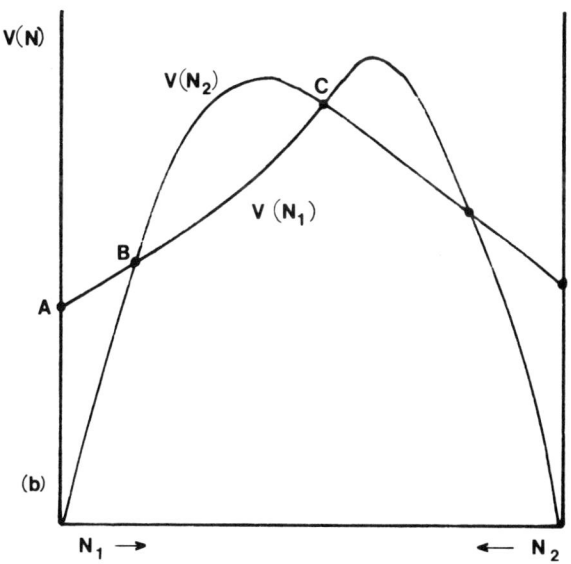

FIGURE 5. Multiple Nash Equilibria: (a) Equilibrium A with all population on one island is stable but Pareto inferior to equilibrium B. (b) Pareto superior equilibrium C is unstable while equilibrium B is stable. (c) Equilibria A and B are stable while equilibrium C is unstable.

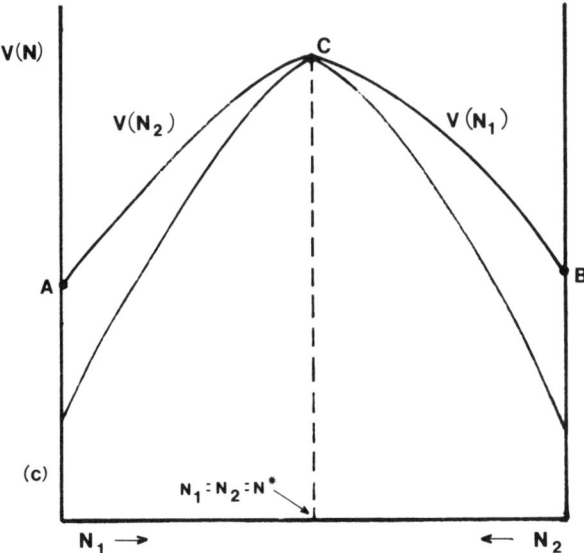

FIGURE 5c.

a much less satisfactory beach could be constructed on the second island. Conversely, an artificial hill for skiing could be constructed on the first island; but on the second, only a minimal amount of expenditure is required for the development of a ski resort. If, by chance, the skiers happened to settle on the first island and the swimmers on the second, then there could be an inefficient Nash equilibrium. Given that the ski resort has not been developed on the second island, the skiers prefer their artificial hill; and given that the beach has not been developed on the first island, the swimmers prefer their little scrawny beach. And given the set of individuals who live within each island, the allocation of resources among public and private goods is efficient.

More complicated versions of this matching problem in the version of the model without land can easily be constructed. For example, suppose that there are two types of labor, doctors and lawyers, and four possible types of public goods, A, B, C, and D. There are two types of doctors, with utility functions

$$U^\alpha = u(c) + G_A + \lambda G_B,$$
$$U^\beta = u(c) + G_C + \lambda G_D.$$

Similarly, there are two types of lawyers, with

$$U^\alpha = u(c) + G_A + \lambda G_D,$$
$$U^\beta = u(c) + G_C + \lambda G_B.$$

If all communities mix type α lawyers with type α doctors, and type β lawyers with type β doctors, then there is an equilibrium in which A is produced in the first community and C in the second. But there is another equilibrium in which type α doctors are mixed with type β lawyers, and good B is produced, and type α lawyers are mixed with type β doctors and good D is produced. If $\lambda < 1$, this equilibrium will be Pareto inferior to the former equilibrium.

C. *The Pareto Optimal Allocation with Free Migration May Require Subsidies*

If there is a limited supply of "rich" islands and migration cannot be restricted, then individuals from the "poor" island will migrate to the rich islands until utilities are equalized. This may not be efficient. To see this most vividly, assume there are two types of islands, large islands and small islands. All individuals are identical, and are treated identically. Then the level of utility on any particular island can be expressed as a function of the number of individuals living on that island (assuming that the level of public goods within the island is optimally chosen). The larger island has a larger maximal level of utility. Now assume that, although there is a very large number of such islands, there are too few to accommodate the entire population, if each island is optimally populated. The equal utility equilibrium will require more than the optimal population in the larger island. But note that if the larger island subsidizes the smaller island, the utility level attained at each population size in the representative small island is increased, and in the representative large island it is lowered, but as Figure 6 makes clear, the *equilibrium* level of utility on both islands may be raised and everybody may be better off as a result of the subsidy. If there are only two islands (which stretches the plausibility of some of the other assumptions in the analysis), then it makes sense for the large (rich) island to subsidize the small (poor) island, but in the general case, where there are many large (rich) islands, any single island is likely to believe it will have a negligible effect on the supply of potential migrants.

The misallocation of individuals resulting from differences in endowments of different communities is a problem of

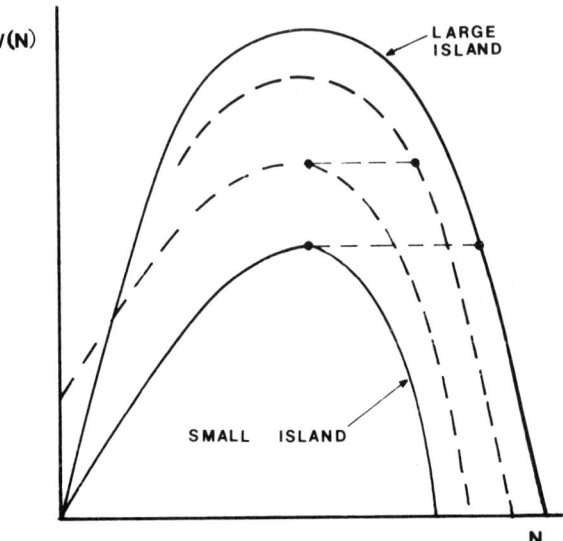

FIGURE 6. Equilibria with different types of islands. A subsidy from the large (rich) island to the small (poor) island generates a Pareto improvement.

some practical importance. If Alberta decides to use its oil revenues to supply public goods, then it may attract migration beyond the efficient level. Some of the potential consumer surplus may be appropriated by owners of land in Alberta in the form of higher land rents; nonetheless, there is no presumption that the equilibrium level of migration will be efficient. Indeed, the major effect of the higher land rents may be to make Alberta more attractive to those who have a low preference for consuming land, which need not be in accord with the Pareto efficient allocation of labor. Alberta could, of course, effectively discriminate between current inhabitants and future migrants by distributing ownership claims in the oil to current inhabitants. This would eliminate the source of the inefficiency. Individuals would no longer have an incentive to migrate to Alberta to capture a share of the "public" rents associated with the oil.

D. *Community Developers*

The problems discussed in Sections IV.A and IV.B can be alleviated by introducing town entrepreneurs (community developers). Although there may well not be an equilibrium with community developers (the core of the economy may be empty), it is clear that when the economy is at an inefficient Nash equilibrium there is scope for a community developer to enter, reorganize the allocation of labor, and appropriate for himself the surplus that is thereby generated. The critical question, however, is whether the developer will be able to appropriate a sufficiently large fraction of the surplus to compensate him. In the non-land-based version of the model, a developer might propose to the members of two (or more) communities a rearrangement that would make all of them better off. Once they perceive this rearrangement, the developer's services may no longer be needed; the citizens within the communities simply appropriate the increased returns for themselves.

This is, of course, a standard problem: the public good is a public good. It may be very difficult for any individual to appropriate the returns from pursuing the public good. Moses led his people to the promised land, but was unable to enjoy any of the fruits of his public service; the problem which beset Moses has beset others who have labored in the public service.

In certain situations, public good problems can be resolved, or at least alleviated, by establishing the appropriate property rights. In the case of what we have referred to as "land-based communities," the landowners as a group may benefit from improving the efficiency with which public services are provided and from providing public goods which are more in accord with the preferences of the inhabitants. Even then, however, each landowner has an incentive to "free ride" on the efforts put forth by other landowners. In the next section, we show that maximizing land values will not, in general, lead to Pareto efficient equilibria. Nonetheless, there are important incentives for landowners to make sure that public goods are efficiently provided. In contrast, we show in Section VI that not only do renters not have any incentives for ensuring that public goods be efficiently provided, but they may have perverse incentives to ensure that the kinds of public goods that are provided are unattractive to those who might be considering immigrating into the community.

V. LAND CAPITALIZATION

One of the important implications of free migration is that if there are differences among communities in public goods, amenities, or taxes, these differences should be reflected (capitalized) in the value of land. This in turn has important implications for the supply of public goods as individuals in a community are concerned not only with the direct consumption benefits associated with any expenditure-tax program, but also with the effects of the program on land values. Thus, an individual in a community with good schools who has no children may still be concerned that the schools in his community maintain their quality, lest property values decline.

Two questions then arise: (1) What implications does this have for the kinds of public goods-taxes each individual within a community votes for? and (2) What implications does this, in turn, have for the local public goods equilibrium?

The questions have a clear parallel to those asked in the theory of the firm: (1) Under what conditions will shareholders wish the firm to maximize their market value? and (2) What implications does firm market value maximization have for the efficiency of market equilibrium?

In traditional competitive theory, when there is a complete set of markets and each shareholder in each firm takes the prices of all goods as given, then all shareholders will wish all firms to maximize their stock market value; in doing so, firms will ensure the efficiency of the economy. When there is not a complete set of markets, as in the traditional monopolistically competitive model, the prices faced by any (even small) firm may alter as it changes, for instance, its production decisions. In that case, it can be shown that the shareholders may not wish to maximize stock market value, there will not be unanimity among the shareholders about what the firm should do, and even if the firm were to maximize stock market value, the market allocation would not in general be Pareto efficient (see, for instance, Stiglitz, 1972; Grossman and Stiglitz, 1980).

Exactly parallel results obtain here. In our discussion of Section III, we considered the case where there is a sufficiently large number of communities that each community takes the level of utility of each type of individual as given. If the owners of the land can choose to live in other communities and still obtain the rents on their land, it is clear that, since their opportunity set is unambiguously increased by having their land rents maximized, they will wish to choose the level of public goods in such a way as to maximize net rents; our earlier analysis established in that situation that the level of public goods will, in fact, be Pareto efficient.

But if individuals lose their rights to obtain rents when they emigrate, then clearly individuals will be concerned not only with land rents, but with the supply of public goods provided within their community. They will not wish the community to maximize net land rents.

More generally, if there are sufficiently few communities that there are some infra-marginal individuals (*i.e.*, some individuals who would not migrate were taxes raised slightly or the level of public goods decreased slightly), then there will not be unanimity among the citizens on what policy the government should pursue; not everyone will wish the community to maximize land rents. Moreover, maximizing land rents will not, in general, be Pareto efficient.

The critical element in the determination of land values is the valuation of the marginal person not living in the community. Communities increase their land values by making themselves more attractive to those not presently living in them. Thus, if there is a large number of communities with inhabitants identical in characteristics to those in the given community, then the marginal migrants are identical to the present inhabitants. Making the community more attractive to these marginal migrants improves the welfare of the current inhabitants.

When, however, every community differs slightly from every other one, then the marginal migrant is distinctly different from the current inhabitants. This has an important effect on those planning to sell their land. Thus an "older voter" more concerned with the value of his land will vote for a public goods package which is more attractive to younger potential migrants who are on the margin of entering. As a result, the equilibrium will reflect more the preference of the median individual within the society than the median individual within the community. Not surprisingly, then, the equilibrium which emerges is not in general Pareto optimal (see Stiglitz, 1974a; Atkinson and Stiglitz, 1980).[18,19]

---

[18]*Even when individuals differ only by age, and not by tastes, the market equilibrium may not be Pareto optimal. Assume, for instance, that there were two techniques for producing a public good, one using current resources, the other using capital resources. Assume that only the young benefit directly from the public good (schools); the old only benefit indirectly from the effect on market values. Assume, moreover, that we cannot differentiate taxes on the basis of age, and that mobility costs are sufficiently high that all communities are mixtures of the young and the old. The old will then always prefer the capital resource method of producing the public good since that is the only way that they can appropriate the returns. This will be so even if it is the less efficient way of producing the public good.*

[19]*We have focused on changes within a single community. Should property owners support a national program which increases the supply of public goods that could be obtained*

It should be noted that the change in land rents does not, in general, provide an accurate estimate of the benefits accruing, for instance, from an improved transportation network, a more efficient public administration, or a better allocation of public goods (see Arnott and Stiglitz, 1979). Assume, for instance, that some community discovered a way of producing community services at lower cost; it could then provide the same public goods services with lower taxes. This would induce those not living in the community to move in; immigration continues until land values rise to the point where the marginal migrant is indifferent to staying in his original community. Thus, if land values increased by an amount equal to the present discounted value of the tax savings, and plot sizes were fixed, equilibrium would be restored. But if plot sizes were variable, the higher value of land would induce individuals to purchase smaller plot sizes; thus, for any *discrete* tax reduction, the equilibrating increase in land values exceeds the present discounted value of the tax reduction.

The analysis so far has assumed that all land within the community is homogeneous. In fact, of course, different parcels of land are quite different, and what is in the interests of one landowner may not be in the interests of another. For instance, after a set of apartments is constructed near the urban center, it is in the interests of those apartment owners to pass a zoning law restricting further construction of apartments. Such a restriction increases the wealth of those who presently own land on which apartments have already been constructed, at the same time that it decreases the wealth of those who presently own land on which apartments would have been constructed in the absence of the zoning restrictions. One group of landowners, in effect, has managed to confiscate part of the wealth of another group of landowners. Their incentives for attempting to do so are clear, in spite of the fact that there may be significant deadweight losses as a result. (Direct confiscation, a more efficient way of transferring resources from one group to another, may not be allowed by the political process.)

Similarly, renters have an interest in attempting to confiscate the wealth of the owners of land (and buildings).

---

from a fixed rate of property taxes? Such a change would increase or decrease property values depending on whether the increased effective supply of public goods increases or decreases the demand for land. The effects of changes in land rents when all communities change, say, their level of public goods are thus markedly different from the effects which occur when only one community alters its behavior.

The means by which they do this, and the consequences for the nature of the local public goods equilibrium, are the subject of the next section.

VI. RENTAL CAPITALIZATION

The benefits of public goods are reflected not only in land values, but also in rents. Since in certain large cities renters comprise a majority of the population, it is important to understand how various public goods-tax programs affect their welfare.

Consider, first, public goods programs financed by land taxes. (The other cases follow along similar lines.) In deciding to migrate, renters are concerned with the wage they receive (after tax), the level of public goods and the level of rents. Thus the level of land taxation is in itself of no interest. An improvement in the efficiency with which public services are provided (keeping the level of public services unchanged) leaves renters completely unaffected. Thus, they will have no concern for the efficiency of public services. Moreover, an improvement in the quality of public services will be immediately reflected in the rents they have to pay, provided there is an infinite number of potential immigrants identical to themselves; if not, the sole concern of the renter in evaluating any program is whether it raises rents by less than it improves his welfare (lowers rents by more than it decreases his welfare). Thus, a renter who has a less than average aversion to garbage in city streets will vote for a small expenditure on garbage collection; although he would like more garbage collection, he realizes that any increase will be more than offset by rent increases. Indeed, he may even vote for something he dislikes, knowing that others dislike it even more.

Thus, renters have no incentive to ensure that public services are provided efficiently, and have perverse incentives with regard to the choice of quality and quantity of public goods.

VII. REDISTRIBUTION

One of the most noted aspects of community formation in the United States is the important role that income-wealth differences play. This is not surprising, as individuals with different incomes are likely to have different attitudes towards public and private goods. There are, however, two important implications of free migration related to wealth differences.

First, we noted in our basic result on the optimality of the local public goods competitive equilibrium that there was effectively no scope for income redistribution. Any attempt by a community to redistribute income away from some group would simply induce migration. Although the assumptions of that model are quite extreme, it is clear that the *power to redistribute income locally with free migration is severely limited*.

Second, in situations where immigration cannot be restricted, and discriminatory taxes against the poor cannot be imposed, there may be some incentive for the poor to migrate into the rich communities. In the case of pure public goods, this may be of little concern: there is no extra cost associated with the poor being (relatively) free riders on the rich provided that the political structure does not lead to an allocation of resources to the public good which is different from that which the rich would have chosen by themselves, and provided there are not congestion effects. If there are, then the rich may still wish to exclude the poor.

In the case of publicly provided private goods--such as education--there is a real cost to the rich of having more poor individuals living within their community. The rich will thus attempt to exclude the poor. There are a wide variety of exclusionary devices, for example, requiring large minimum size lots, having a very high property tax rate (so the poor cannot *afford* to live in the community), or having a very low property tax rate with a correspondingly very low level of public services (both rich and poor individuals can substitute private for public goods, but the poor can do this less successfully). Although such exclusionary devices clearly create distortions relative to the first best optimum where poor individuals could be directly excluded or discriminatory taxation could be imposed, the existence of these exclusionary practices does not imply that the local public goods equilibrium is not a constrained Pareto optimum, taking into account the restrictions which are, in fact, imposed on the set of instruments which the communities can employ to discriminate. Moreover, introducing further restrictions on the set of exclusionary devices (*e.g.*, not allowing certain zoning requirements) may simply lead to the substitution of less efficient and desirable exclusionary devices. Such restrictions may lead to a Pareto inferior local public goods equilibrium.

The Theory of Local Public Goods

VIII. THE DECENTRALIZATION OF PARETO EFFICIENT ALLOCATIONS

The previous sections established that, while there were some extremely restrictive conditions under which a local public goods competitive equilibrium might be Pareto efficient, there was a strong presumption that it was not. This established that the first of the two Fundamental Theorems of Welfare Economics did not extend to economies in which there were local public goods. We now consider the second theorem: Can every Pareto efficient allocation be decentralized? We show that, in general, not every Pareto efficient allocation can be decentralized. Since many of the arguments employed to show this are straightforward modifications of earlier arguments which showed that the market allocation was inefficient, our discussion will be very brief.

There are four problems with the decentralizability of the set of Pareto optimal allocations with free migration:

(1) There may only be a single community. The fact that with *pure* public goods the marginal cost of an additional individual enjoying the public good is zero leads to a strong presumption that there be a single community. There are two grounds for forming separate communities.

(a) The public good is not a pure public good; there is congestion in its use. (At the extreme, it may be a publicly provided private good, for which the marginal cost of usage is equal to the average cost.) Most of the public goods which are presently provided by local communities fall within this category--education, sewage, garbage collection, *etc*. And this is the category of goods which Tiebout seems to have had in mind. Yet, these are not the pure public goods which Samuelson (1954) described, and thus Tiebout's analysis does not provide a resolution of the public goods problems posed there.

(b) There are diminishing returns in private goods in the formation of larger communities. This may be either because of diminishing returns to production (as in the "island" model described above), or because of increased transport costs as communities in which the public good is provided centrally become larger.

Even when there are diminishing returns, it may not be desirable to form separate communities; there must be sufficiently rapidly diminishing returns. Consider a simple economy in which the output of goods is a function of the number of individuals living in the community. For simplicity, assume all individuals are treated the same. Assume, as before, that a unit of output can be used to produce either a unit of the private good or a unit of the public good.

Thus, for a fixed population, the production possibilities schedule appears as in Figures 7a and 7b. If we increase the population, we can increase the supply of public goods (G), but decrease the per capita supply of private goods (c). Thus, the production possibilities schedule, the outer envelope of these linear schedules, is convex. Whether it is desirable to have a finite or infinite number of people in the community depends on the utility function for public and private goods (see Figures 7a and 7b).

These non-convexities have one further important implication. Even when it is desirable to have more than one community, it is quite likely that there may not be a sufficiently large number of communities that the utility-taking analogue to the perfectly competitive model is likely to be more akin to a monopolistically competitive model, as discussed in Sections IV-VI.

(2) The public good must be localized. Obviously, if the level of public goods provided in one community affects the level of welfare of citizens in another, we cannot decentralize the provision of public goods. Each community will undersupply public goods. Again, many of the most important public goods (e.g., the benefits of research and development, much of the programming for television, etc.) are all *national* public goods and cannot be localized. This further limits the scope of the Tiebout model for providing a resolution to the problems associated with the provision of public goods.

(3) The Pareto optimal allocation cannot entail subsidies from the citizens of one community to those of another. The conventional statement of the second welfare theorem asserts that every Pareto optimal allocation can be sustained by a competitive economy with the appropriate *lump sum* redistributions. Thus, in the present context, the parallel theorem requires that any redistributions not be contingent upon the individual's choice of location.

We established earlier that, in the land-based model, Pareto optimal allocations (with free migration) will require inter-island transfers, unless all islands are identical. Lump sum taxes and subsidies (which are not dependent on the individual's location) are not sufficient.[20]

[20]*In this situation, a form of "regionalization" may be possible; that is, a collection of islands, large and small, in the appropriate proportion, can enjoy fiscal autonomy from all other islands. This region is just a miniaturization of the economy as a whole. Under more general circumstances, where all islands differ, then even the partial decentralization associated with regionalization may not support the Pareto optimal allocation.*

The Theory of Local Public Goods

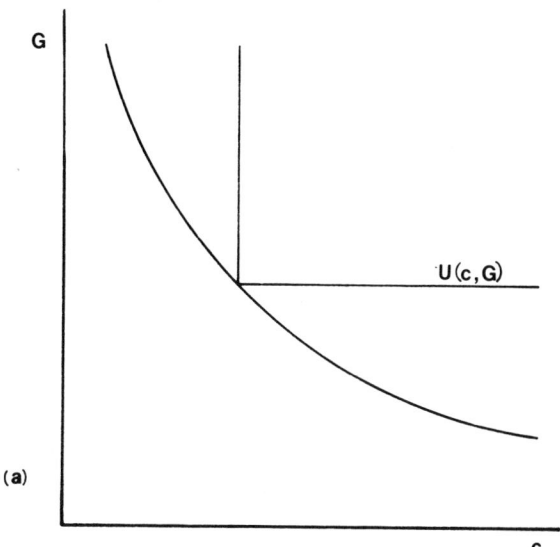

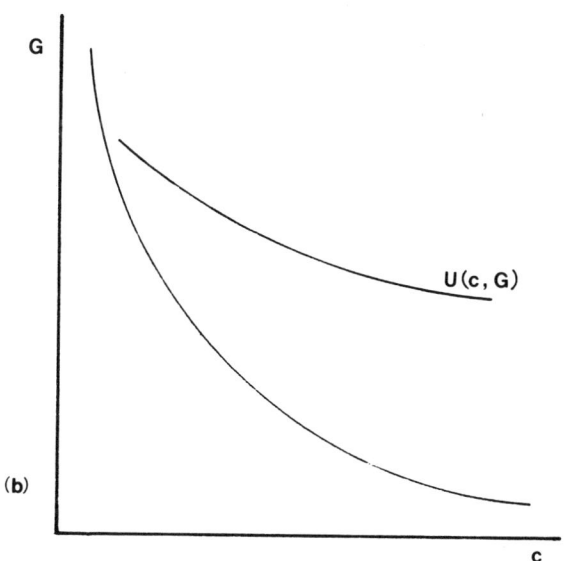

FIGURE 7. Optimal number of communities: (a) Finite number of communities is optimal. (b) Single community is optimal.

(4) If the number of individuals is not an exact multiple of the optimal size of a community, then if there is community entrepreneurship, the Pareto optimal allocation may not be supported by a decentralized equilibrium. A community entrepreneur is someone who organizes a new community, with a new set of rules for the determination of the level of consumption of private goods as a function of the endowments of factors he brings to the community. Consider, for instance, the land-based model introduced earlier. Then in Figure 5a the Pareto optimal equal utilities equilibrium entails both communities being below the optimal size. A community entrepreneur could then propose forming a new community of the optimal size; he could appropriate as rents a sufficient amount to make individuals indifferent to migrating. Though this itself would not be an equilibrium if there is a competitive supply of entrepreneurs, it does establish that the Pareto optimal allocation cannot itself be sustained.

IX. CONCLUSION

In this paper, I have argued that the Fundamental Theorems of Welfare Economics do not extend to economies with local public goods; the conditions required to ensure that every Pareto optimum can be generated by a competitive local public goods equilibrium (with appropriate lump sum redistributions), and those required to ensure that the competitive local public goods equilibrium be Pareto optimal are indeed stringent.[21]

At a theoretical level, this should not be surprising as the presence of local public goods introduces a non-convexity, and non-convexities are often troublesome for competitive theory since: (a) competitive equilibrium may not exist; (b) non-convexities in practice are likely to be associated with various kinds of imperfectly (monopolistically) competitive behavior; and (c) where there are non-convexities, it is not necessarily the case that every Pareto-efficient allocation can be supported by a competitive equilibrium with appropriate lump sum redistributions.

[21]*Throughout this paper, I have assumed perfect information on the part of consumers about the packages of goods offered by different communities. Recent work in competitive equilibrium theory has shown how critical the perfect information assumption is to the optimality results that have been obtained. The assumption of perfect information about public goods (e.g., schools) of potential migrants seems particularly questionable (see Hannaway and Garner, 1982).*

The Theory of Local Public Goods

Perhaps more significantly, while the conditions under which the efficiency of the local public goods equilibrium can be established are far more general than those conventionally assumed (admitting, for instance, heterogeneity both in skills and tastes), some of the instances of "market failure" we have observed correspond to important policy issues; we have noted, for instance, the possibility of equilibria with excessive concentration of population, and pointed out that, while there are instances where the existence of land developers might lead to welfare improvements, there are other instances where market value maximization does not lead to Pareto optimal allocation of resources.

More disturbingly, we have noted the absence of appropriate incentives on the part of renters for voting for efficient public goods-tax packages. (Landowners benefit, of course, from better public goods-tax programs, but there, the free rider problem implies that it is not in the interest of any single individual to ensure that the public good is done.)[22]

The inefficiencies we have noted in the competitive local public goods equilibrium provide some arguments for the role of regional and national authorities in the provision of local public goods and in redistribution across communities.[23]

Still, I believe that this discussion vastly underestimates the virtues of a decentralized mechanism for providing public goods.[24] Local communities can respond to local variability more effectively than centralized control (although it is a moot question whether centralized control at the state level is more responsive to local needs than centralized control at the national level). The opportunities for political participation and choice (voice and exit) provided by local communities are of value themselves in a democratic

---

[22]*In the private market, when a firm is inefficiently run, there may be an incentive for a takeover. Although it is conceivable that a community organizer would buy all the land in a community, change the management, and make a profit, in practice this does not occur. Even for private firms, the efficacy of the takeover mechanism has been questioned. A shareholder, believing that the firm is about to be taken over and a more efficient management installed, might well refuse to sell his shares, preferring to realize the capital gain himself.*

[23]*The design of optimal interventions is a question I hope to pursue on another occasion.*

[24]*Just as I have argued that the conventional competitive paradigm does not accurately reflect the virtues (and vices) of the market (Stiglitz, 1982).*

society. Even if voters have limited incentives for ensuring that the public good is pursued, local administrators have incentives for demonstrating innovativeness and efficiency. (Their incentives are still only loosely related to the preferences of their constituents, but similar arguments apply to firm managers.)

The opportunities for extending the scope of choice and competition within the public sector have not yet been fully exploited. The question before us is, recognizing that such competition does not necessarily lead to efficient resource allocations, how competition and choice can be introduced to best serve the public interest.

REFERENCES

Arnott, R. J., and J. E. Stiglitz, 1979. "Aggregate Land Rents, Expenditure on Public Goods and Optimal City Size," *Quarterly Journal of Economics* 63:471-500.
Atkinson, A. B., and J. E. Stiglitz, 1980. *Lectures in Public Economics*. New York and London: McGraw-Hill.
Berglas, E., 1976. "Distribution of Tastes and Skills and the Provision of Local Public Goods," *Journal of Public Economics* 6:409-423.
Buchanan, J., and C. J. Goetz, 1972. "Efficiency Limits of Fiscal Mobility: An Assessment of the Tiebout Model," *Journal of Public Economics* 1:25-43.
Dixit, A. K., and J. E. Stiglitz, 1977. "Monopolistic Competition and Optimum Product Diversity," *American Economic Review* 67:297-308.
Flatters, F., V. Henderson, and P. Mieszkowski, 1974. "Public Goods, Efficiency, and Regional Fiscal Equalization," *Journal of Public Economics* 2:99-112.
Grossman, S., and J. E. Stiglitz, 1980. "Stockholder Unanimity in the Making of Production and Financial Decisions," *Quarterly Journal of Economics* 94:543-566.
Groves, T., and J. Ledyard, 1977. "Optimal Allocation of Public Goods: A Solution to the 'Free-Rider' Problem," *Econometrica* 45:783-809.
Hannaway, J., and W. Garner, 1982. "Private Schools: The Client Connection," in Michael E. Manley-Kasimir (ed.), *Family Choice in Schooling*. Lexington, Mass.: Lexington Books.
Kramer, G., 1973. "On a Class of Equilibrium Conditions for Majority Rule," *Econometrica* 41:285-297.
Lancaster, K. J., 1975. "Socially Optimal Product Differentiation," *American Economic Review* 65:567-585.

Pestieau, P., 1980. "Fiscal Mobility and Local Public Goods: A Survey of the Empirical and Theoretical Studies of the Tiebout Model," Université Catholique de Louvain, Louvain-la-Neuve, Belgium, Research Program: Spatial Analysis and Public Services Policy, Paper No. 6.

Salop, S. C., 1979. "Monopolistic Competition with Outside Goods," *Bell Journal of Economics* 10:141-156.

Samuelson, P. A., 1954. "The Pure Theory of Public Expenditures," *Review of Economics and Statistics* 36:387-389.

Slutsky, S. M., 1977. "A Voting Model for the Allocation of Public Goods: Existence of an Equilibrium," *Journal of Economic Theory* 14:299-325.

Spence, A. M., 1976. "Product Selection, Fixed Costs, and Monopolistic Competition," *Review of Economic Studies* 43: 217-235.

Stiglitz, J. E., 1972. "On the Optimality of the Stock Market Allocation of Investment," *Quarterly Journal of Economics* 86:25-60.

Stiglitz, J. E., 1974a. "Demand for Education in Public and Private School Systems," *Journal of Public Economics* 3: 349-386.

Stiglitz, J. E., 1974b. "Incentives and Risk Sharing in Sharecropping," *Review of Economic Studies* 41:219-255.

Stiglitz, J. E., 1975. "Incentives, Risk, and Information: Notes Towards a Theory of Hierarchy," *Bell Journal of Economics and Management Science* 6:552-579.

Stiglitz, J. E., 1977. "The Theory of Local Public Goods," in M. S. Feldstein and R. P. Inman (eds.), *The Economics of Public Services*. London: Macmillan.

Stiglitz, J. E., 1982. "Utilitarianism and Horizontal Equity: The Case for Random Taxation," *Journal of Public Economics* 18:1-33.

Stiglitz, J. E., forthcoming-a. "Information and Competition," *Oxford Economic Papers*.

Stiglitz, J. E., forthcoming-b. "Public Goods in Open Economies with Heterogeneous Individuals," *Journal of Public Economics*.

Stiglitz, J. E., forthcoming-c. "Variety, Equity, and Efficiency and the Theory of Monopolistic Competition," *Journal of Political Economy*.

Tiebout, C. M., 1956. "A Pure Theory of Local Expenditures," *Journal of Political Economy* 64:416-424.

Vickrey, W., 1977. "The City as a Firm," in M. S. Feldstein and R. P. Inman (eds.), *The Economics of Public Services*. London: Macmillan.

Chapter 3

BEYOND TIEBOUT: MODELING THE POLITICAL ECONOMY
OF LOCAL GOVERNMENT

Susan Rose-Ackerman

School of Law
Columbia University
New York, New York

I. INTRODUCTION

Doing two things at once is difficult. Models in which people both vote and buy can easily become intractable and opaque. Yet the integration of political and economic models must be a central concern of modern political economy. One area where integration has been attempted is in the study of multiple government systems where people can move between jurisdictions. Multiple government models were first proposed by Tiebout (1956) not as a way of integrating politics and economics, but as a way of avoiding the political problems of public choice. His article was a response to Samuelson's (1954) claim that a decentralized market system could not efficiently provide "public" goods.[1] Tiebout and Samuelson, along with Musgrave (1959, Chapter 6), believed that the problem of preference revelation was central to political-economic analysis. Their work did not explicitly consider the possibility that even a government with perfect knowledge about preferences might not choose the "optimal" solution. Tiebout's contribution (following Margolis, 1955) was to point out that many publicly provided services are not pure Samuelsonian public goods. Instead, the marginal cost

---

[1]*Samuelson defined pure public goods as those consumed in common so that the addition of one more consumer has no impact on the consumption of anyone else.*

of adding consumers is not always zero. The services become congested above some optimal scale so that the marginal cost of adding more consumers is ultimately positive and increasing. Tiebout then went on to posit a world with many "communities" each producing a different level of public services and levying a head tax on residents. People could move freely between communities so long as the towns had not attained optimal scale. These "towns" each somehow chose a fixed level of public services, and households based their own choices only on the tax-spending combination of each town. There was no land, no housing market, and no commuting across jurisdictional boundaries to get to work. All household income was from bonds. The problem of preference revelation was solved, just as it is in a competitive private market, by the choices of migrants. With free entry of communities and public services that are technically close to private goods, each "town" could be run by a profit maximizing entrepreneur and an efficient outcome would prevail. Looked at in this way, the model is analogous to recent work on product differentiation except that Tiebout's towns do not pick the level of public services (see Ellickson, 1979b). Tiebout thought it a virtue of his approach that no separate model of public choice was needed. His world is both efficient and apolitical.

One line of economic research has sought to extend Tiebout's model both by developing the underlying analytical structure and by adding realistic complications. Much of the work has been concerned with establishing the existence and stability of equilibrium and with examining its efficiency properties (see the critiques of this research by Bewley, 1981; Pestieau, 1980; and Stiglitz, 1977, and in this volume). Since this research has been carried out by economists, it is not surprising that they have frequently sought either to eliminate politics from their models entirely or to construct very simple models of governmental operation. Section II discusses the former type of model, and Section III assesses the latter.

The basic message that I draw from past work, however, is that neither strategy will continue to yield useful results. The last decade's work by economists has only served to emphasize the wide range of conditions under which a model of local political choice will be important. The economist's dream of doing away with politics cannot be realized even in the local government context. It is now imperative to develop richer models of local political processes.

In attempting to do this, one turns to the work of other social scientists for guidance. Not surprisingly, one finds that each field has modeled the behavior of governments to give primacy to its own discipline. Thus, both sociologists and economists have tried to develop models of local government that eliminate the need for political science. While economists have drawn analogies between a local government system and a competitive market, sociologists have developed a "stratification" theory that emphasizes the importance of social structure in determining political choice. Polsby (1980), a political scientist, argues in turn that this branch of sociological research on local government is limited by its failure to consider politics. He argues in favor of cross-disciplinary research that will link the work of political scientists and sociologists. However, just as economists have taken no account of research in political science and sociology on community power, so Polsby, in defending the "pluralist" theory and methods[2] used in his own work and in that of Dahl (1961) and Wolfinger (1974), does not discuss economic research on local government. The word "economic" is used along with the word "elite" to describe wealthy people or people who work for important business firms or banks. Economics understood as a theory of choice subject to constraints is not considered. This neglect of economics occurs because in both the sociological and the political science literature, the city is commonly viewed as a closed system. It may interact with higher levels of government or try to impose costs on nearby suburbs, but the mobility of households and firms has not been systematically linked to the political choices of local governments. These gaps in past research suggest that one should ask how previously unrelated research in sociology, political science, and economics might be usefully brought together. Section IV points out several ways in which this integration might be accomplished.

II. THE LIMITS OF TIEBOUT MODELS: HOW FAR CAN ONE PUSH THE COMPETITIVE ANALOGY?

A. *Models of Efficient, Competitive Systems*

A multiple government system has little normative appeal if everyone has the same tastes and incomes and if the government apparatus is controlled by voters. Then, there are no gains from having more than one government unless a single government cannot operate as efficiently as a decen-

[2]*"Pluralism" is not a term with a precise, simple meaning, but it refers, in general, to the proposition that power is dispersed in political systems among a variety of groups and individuals. See Polsby (1980).*

tralized system. However, even if tastes and incomes vary, two extreme assumptions can be made about public services, either one of which will eliminate any first-best justification for a multiple government system. On the one hand, we can assume that governments produce pure Samuelsonian public goods with no congestion and that Lindahl taxes[3] are possible. Then, no matter how different are people's tastes, a pattern of taxes and spending can always be found so that a unitary government dominates a multiple government system for every citizen. On the other hand, we can assume that local public goods are really publicly provided private goods. Then, it would in general be efficient simply to turn over the production of these services to private entrepreneurs.

As soon as these extreme assumptions are relaxed, a multiple government system can be efficient so long as tastes and incomes differ. Suppose, for example, that Lindahl taxes are possible but that local public services are neither purely public nor purely private. In other words, there are scale economies with respect to population, but at some point congestion occurs so that the marginal cost of adding an extra consumer eventually becomes positive and increasing. Therefore, it will be efficient to place people in communities large enough so that scale economies are exhausted but not so large that congestion arises. Alternatively, even if the services are Samuelsonian public goods with no congestion, it may not be possible to set Lindahl taxes. Suppose, for example, that everyone in a given jurisdiction must face the same tax bill. In this second-best world, welfare might be improved by grouping people by their tastes for public services.

Once it has been established that a multiple government system is preferable to a unitary system on efficiency grounds, then one must determine, as a positive matter, whether a stable, efficient equilibrium actually exists. One way in which this can be done is to assume that people fall into a finite number of taste and income classes and that congestion effects make it efficient to assign each taste and

[3]*Lindahl taxes are set individually for each person so that the government's budget balances, the sum of the marginal rates of substitution of public for private goods equals the marginal cost, and, given his or her tailor-made tax-price, each individual would choose just the level of public services that is actually provided. The obvious difficulty with such a tax scheme is the problem of giving people an incentive to reveal their preferences truthfully. For an accessible discussion, see Feldman (1980, pp. 112-119).*

income class to a different community (see, for example, Ellickson, 1979b; McGuire, 1974; Stiglitz, 1977; Bewley, 1981). Ignoring the link between land or housing markets and local government choices, these "club" models produce a world where unanimity prevails within each community, and there are no marginal citizens. The discrete number of taste and income classes and the conditions placed on the production function and the tax system interact to produce an equilibrium where everyone strictly prefers his or her own community to all others. Even here, however, other stable but inefficient equilibria may exist with a heterogeneous population in each community (see Bewley, 1981; Brueckner, 1979; Pestieau, 1980). For example, suppose there are two towns and ten people with high demands for public services and ten with low demands who must be allocated to two towns. Then, ignoring the process of political choice and assuming that everyone acts independently, there could be two stable equilibria. In the first, high demanders all occupy one community and low demanders occupy the other. In the second, each town contains five of each type of person and produces identical levels of public services. History or luck could determine which pattern prevails, and costless migration would do nothing to induce society to shift from the second equilibrium to the first. (For other examples of inefficient equilibria, see Stiglitz, 1977).

An equilibrium where each town has a homogeneous population, and each town's population is different from the population in other towns, is an easy case for two reasons. First, no one is on the margin. Thus, the fiscal externalities isolated by Buchanan and Goetz (1972) and Flatters, Henderson, and Mieszkowski (1974) are not important.[4] Second, the public choice problem within each town is a trivial exercise in maximizing the utility of a representative citizen subject to constraints.

[4]*In Flatters, Henderson, and Mieszkowski (1974), workers are identical but regions have different amounts of land. Then, an efficient equilibrium will only occur if taxes per worker are identical in each region, and this result requires a unitary price elasticity of demand for public goods in terms of private goods. In general, inefficiency occurs because migrants look at average tax prices and do not take account of the effect of their migration on others' tax payments. These fiscal externalities are different from the externalities discussed by Brainard and Dolbear (1967) and Williams (1966) who analyze direct spillovers of benefits and costs between communities. To use Brainard and Dolbear's imagery, each town produces birds some of which fly away to neighboring communities.*

Richter (forthcoming) and Ellickson (1979a) have proved that an equilibrium exists in more general cases where each town's population can be heterogeneous. However, their results provide little support for those who wish to argue that efficient equilibria exist in realistic local government contexts. Richter's equilibria are only "locally" efficient in the sense that *given* the assignment of people to communities, there is no way to make someone better off without making others worse off. Ellickson uses techniques developed to prove the existence of an "approximate" competitive equilibrium in models with indivisibilities to prove a similar result in the local government context. However, the force of his results depends upon how close the local government "approximation" is to the competitive case.[5] In spite of Ellickson's optimism about the importance of his results, it would seem that in general the approximation will not be very close. Given the other factors that determine residential location, many households will confront too few effective choices of public service levels for Ellickson's result to apply (see the critique by Pestieau, 1980). Furthermore, neither Richter nor Ellickson has specified a system of political choice that can produce or sustain equilibrium. When each town contains a mixture of people with various tastes, this is a serious weakness. As we shall see, both the way political choices are made and the kinds of information available to people will have important implications for the existence and stability of equilibrium.[6]

The introduction of a housing or land market--especially when combined with a property tax--further complicates the analysis. The impact of government choices on rents and housing values affects voters' preferences for various tax-expenditure packages. Political behavior is conditional on whether voters own or rent property--and the next section will show that this, in general, will require a model of the

---

[5]*In particular, non-convexities in production must be "small" relative to the size of the market (Ellickson, 1979a). Suppose we start with a population with a variety of tastes that is small enough so that scale economies with respect to population are not exhausted. By replicating that population several times, we eventually reach a point where the population is large enough so that scale economies are exhausted. Then, an approximate competitive equilibrium can be found.*

[6]*Furthermore, as Wheaton (1975) has shown, the existence and stability of equilibrium depends on the tax system. In his model, a poll tax produces a stable equilibrium, but neither a proportional income tax nor a Lindahl tax need do so.*

Beyond Tiebout

political process. Yet, at least one researcher (Hamilton, 1975, 1976) wishes to ignore these complexities. He claims that a multiple government system with a housing market can be efficient if zoning is permitted. As Brueckner (1981) has shown, however, Hamilton has made assumptions that produce a model devoid of any of the distinctive features of local government. Thus, government services are private goods publicly produced at constant cost per resident. Average and marginal costs per person are equal. Housing is perfectly elastically supplied, and there is free entry of communities. Given the production function for public goods, this means that any person who cannot find a town that perfectly matches his or her preferences can simply establish a new town. Towns levy a property tax and set a zoning law so that the property tax becomes a benefit tax. People with identical tastes for housing and public services cluster together. The only people who are excluded by zoning are those who are not willing to "pay their way." They are people who would consume smaller amounts of housing and hence pay a tax that is less than the cost of supplying them with services. In Hamilton's (1975) model, the equilibrium is stable and presents no problems of public choice once it is established since each town is homogeneous. Because government services are simply publicly provided private goods, there is no constraint on the number of possible taste classes. Because housing supply is perfectly elastic, there is no capitalization of taxes or spending into housing values across jurisdictions.[7] Thus, owner occupants have no incentive to set tax and public spending levels in order to obtain capital gains. Once any one of these assumptions is dropped, efficiency is no longer guaranteed *and* a political model of local government choice must be specified.[8]

[7]*For sharply contrasting results, consider the model constructed by Pauly (1976). Pauly assumes that housing is perfectly inelastically supplied and inelastically demanded. He specifies the condition for an equilibrium with no capitalization and then demonstrates that this is a very special case.*

[8]*Even when Hamilton (1976) does consider the case of mixed income communities, he retains his other strong assumptions so that an efficient solution can be produced through zoning. Public choice issues are not raised. Edel and Sclar's (1974) model demonstrating that no capitalization will occur has similar difficulties. See the critique in Pauly (1976).*

B. *The Ubiquity of Politics*

Rather than showing the applicability of Tiebout's theory to a world with property taxes and a housing market, Hamilton has only demonstrated the unrealistic nature of the required assumptions. The theory simply is not very robust. Politics cannot be eliminated from local government models without making extremely strong assumptions about the tastes and opportunities facing citizens.[9] In fact, the shape of the production function for public services, the limitations on the tax system, and the variations in tastes and incomes that produced a justification for a multiple government system in the first place also force one to confront the problem of public choice. Furthermore, unlike a competitive market, and in contrast to Hamilton, the entry of new communities is costly. Various combinations of these conditions produce situations where each town contains a heterogeneous mixture of people. Therefore, governments cannot simply maximize the position of the representative individual.

Political disagreements among the residents of each community can arise in a number of different ways. First, suppose that scale economies with respect to population are large, tastes and incomes are broadly dispersed, and Lindahl taxes are not possible. Towns can form and expand costlessly, and there is no land market. Then, in deciding where to live, households realize that the smaller and more homogeneous is a town's population, the higher the per-capita cost of public services. Thus, people may choose to live in heterogeneous communities to take advantage of scale economies. Even if people did fall into a small number of distinct taste and income classes, it would only be fortuitous if the number of people in each class corresponded with the point at which population scale economies were exhausted. Even if we change the above conditions so that Lindahl taxes are possible, it is not obvious that these taxes will be chosen by a heterogeneous community. One still needs to specify a political process that would produce the efficient choice.

Second, we can drop the assumption of population scale economies if we then assume that the entry of new communities is costly and difficult. This is surely a plausible condi-

[9]*Therefore, research on the theory of clubs cannot be uncritically transferred to the urban economics context. This is an important limitation of the discussion of local government models in Sandler and Tschirhart's (1980) recent survey of the theory of clubs. That paper fails to discuss research that deals either with housing markets or with political choice methods.*

tion since existing towns are likely to be closely packed around the central city so that new towns must incorporate on the urban fringe in locations that are less accessible to employment centers. Then, direct entry restrictions rather than production conditions limit the number of towns, and each town is likely to contain a heterogeneous mixture of people.

Third, an explicit and realistic model of the housing market once again emphasizes the importance of politics. A relatively inelastic supply of housing within each community and restrictions on the entry of new communities will combine to produce partial capitalization of public services and tax differences into property values. So long as tastes differ, citizens will not all be indifferent to all locations. So long as the supply of housing in the metropolitan area is somewhat elastic, changed public service conditions in one community will not be exactly canceled by a change in property values in that town unless the town is very small relative to the community as a whole (see Rose-Ackerman, 1977). Thus, differences in consumers' property wealth can now produce different preferred public choices.

Now that we have seen how political disagreements can arise in realistic contexts, we are ready to assess work that makes an explicit attempt to model political choice.

III. EXIT AND VOTING IN LOCAL GOVERNMENT MODELS

A. *Models of Local Politics*

A political-economic analysis of a local government system must deal with two different issues. First, it must specify the procedure by which choices are made, and the information available to political actors. Second, it must determine who makes the choices and isolate the things that matter to these individuals. In particular, if the model includes a land or housing market, it is necessary to specify how capital gains and losses on property enter the calculations of decisionmakers.

Economists feel most comfortable when they can set up a problem as an objective function to be maximized subject to constraints. This is the lead that has been followed in designing political models of local government. Yet, results in social choice theory from Arrow (1951) to more recent work by Kramer (1973), Gibbard (1973), and Satterthwaite (1975) suggest that it is foolish to search for a single general political objective function to be maximized.[10] Thus, in order to develop local government models solvable by techniques familiar to economists, public choice processes must take a very simple form. In practice, this has meant either dictatorship or a direct democracy with majority rule. To assure that majority rule provides determinate results, strong conditions must be placed on individuals' tastes and information. In particular, if tastes are "single peaked," the tastes of the median voter are reflected in the community's decision, and tractable models are possible. If, however, "single-peakedness" or other equally strong conditions are not satisfied, voting cycles will occur that make the modeling task much more complicated.[11] Thus, the models that have been developed, while yielding sharply contrasting results, do not explore a very rich range of possibilities. This is not to say that the research has not yielded useful insights. Nevertheless, existing work demonstrates that even the simplest political choice models may not produce an equilibrium or may be unstable. These public choice models are important because they emphasize dimensions that have been ignored by most political scientists--the link between local public choice and migration and the importance of capital gains and losses in the housing market. Therefore, before moving to a general critique of this research in Section IV, three broad types of models will be evaluated. First, there are majority rule models where voters do not own property. Second, there are majority rule models where voters do own property. Third, there are a variety of monopoly power or dictatorship models.

B. *Majority Rule Models Where Voters Do Not Own Property*

Intercommunity migration changes each town's set of opportunities and each town's set of tastes. Migration both changes the political composition of the community and affects the tax price of public services--either by affecting the tax base or by leading to population scale economies or diseconomies in production. Even when voters' tastes and opportunities are defined to assure that majority rule produces a determinate outcome, no equilibrium need exist and even if one does exist, it may be neither stable nor efficient.

[10] *For a review of this literature, see Feldman (1980).*
[11] *When a voting cycle exists, majority rule will not produce a determinate outcome that is independent of the order in which alternatives are voted on. See Feldman (1980).*

1. A Simple Example. To illustrate how migration changes both tastes and opportunities, consider a simple model without a land market where voters are myopic and think that the population of their town will remain constant. All towns vote at the same moment in time. Voters in community j pick a level of public services, z_j, and taxes must be levied to balance the budget. However, *before* taxes are levied, households survey the set of z_j available and decide where to move on the assumption that no one else will move and that per capita taxes will be unaffected by their choice. Everyone immediately moves to his or her chosen community and must stay there until after the next vote. Thus, if migration occurs, both movers and non-movers find that taxes are higher or lower than they expected, depending both upon whether in or out migration has occurred and on the production function for public services. In the next set of local referenda, people once again myopically assume that population will remain constant.

To take a specific example, suppose that there are 200 people in a society and that 51 relatively low demanders are in one town and 149 relatively high demanders are in another. People can be ranked from 1 to 200 on the basis of the strength of their demand for private versus public goods, where low numbers imply low preferences for public goods. Then, in the first town, the preferences of the median voter, ranked 26, determine the public choice and in the second town, the person ranked 126 is decisive. The public good is purely public and costs $1 per unit. Thus, per capita taxes are expected to be $z_1/51$ in town one and $z_2/149$ in town two, where z_i is the level of public service in i. Even though z_2 is higher, expected per capita taxes may be lower in town two. If this happens, everyone moves to town two and in the next referendum, the choice of the new median voters at positions 100 and 101 dominate. (To assure a determinate solution, we need to assume that 100 and 101 have the same tastes. Otherwise, we need to specify how majority rule operates with an even number of voters.) Consider, however, the less extreme case where $z_2/149 > z_1/51$. Some relatively high demand voters in town one may now decide to move to town two. Per capita taxes in two are then lower than expected. In the next set of referenda, town one reduces z_1 both because its tax base has shrunk and because the median voter is a person with lower tastes for public services. In town two, z_2 may rise or fall. The tax base in two has improved, but the median voter has a lower taste for public services. In either case, the system can gradually unravel until a single town exists.

Now add congestion. Suppose that the cost of producing the public good is $c(z_i, n_i) = z_i + n_i^2$, when n_i is the population of i. Now expected per capita taxes are

$$t_i = (z_i + n_i^2)/n_i = z_i/n_i + n_i.$$

Suppose $z_2 = 3z_1$ when $n_1 = 51$, $n_2 = 149$; then

$$t_1 = z_1/51 + 51, \quad t_2 = 3z_1/149 + 149,$$

or t_2 is approximately $t_1 + 98$. Now migration can go in either direction. Whichever way people move, they may be disappointed rather than pleasantly surprised with the result. If ten people migrate from one to two, actual taxes, $\hat{t}_i$, are $\hat{t}_1 = z_1/41 + 41$, $\hat{t}_2 = 3z_1/159 + 159$. Now we have three possible cases:

Case (1) $\hat{t}_1 > t_1$ and $\hat{t}_2 > t_2$: $7897 > z_1 > 2091$

Case (2) $\hat{t}_1 < t_1$ and $\hat{t}_2 > t_2$: $z_1 < 2091$

Case (3) $\hat{t}_1 > t_1$ and $\hat{t}_2 < t_2$: $z_1 > 7897$.

Case (3) is the same as the result with no congestion and is a potentially unstable situation where migration from one to two raises realized taxes in one and lowers them in two. In Case (2), migration from one to two in one period may produce migration from two to one after the next referendum. In Case (1), the implications for long-term migration are ambiguous since taxes are higher than expected in both towns.

2. *More General Models*. The example described above is similar to the more general model developed by Westhoff (1977, 1979) that also has no land market. Westhoff analyzes a situation where tastes are "continuous." The population is represented by a frequency function defined over people's marginal rates of substitution between public and private goods where the ranking of consumers is the same for all public good-tax rate combinations. Thus, someone with a relatively strong preference for public versus private goods in one choice situation will have the same position in the ranking of consumers in all other choice situations (Westhoff, 1979). Each government is a mechanism that collects taxes and balances its budget each period by efficiently spending all taxes on public services. There is one kind of government service and one kind of private good. The tax system is exogenously fixed so that each government must levy a proportional income tax on its residents. Westhoff assumes that migrants do not take account of the effect of migration on communities' tax-expenditure choices. Similarly, voters do not take account of the way public sector choices may

affect migration. Therefore, in the normal case with smooth convex preferences, each voter has a most preferred level of public services, taking into account the tax payments that accompany each choice, and utility falls off monotonically as public services increase or decrease. These assumptions guarantee that within any town with a fixed population, preferences are single-peaked, and majority rule voting produces a unique outcome. The restrictions on both the tax system and the number of goods permit majority rule to "work" by reducing the public choice problem to one dimension. In equilibrium with a fixed number of communities, the political choices of each community must produce a pattern of public services where no one wants to migrate.

Westhoff (1979) shows that when people can be unambiguously ranked by their relative preferences for public goods *and* when all marginal rates of substitution are represented so there are no "holes" in the preference distribution, then an equilibrium exists with a fixed number of communities. If, however, there are "holes" in the preference distribution, then no equilibrium need exist. Furthermore, even if an equilibrium does exist it may well be unstable.[12] Clearly, it is irrelevant to discuss the optimality of a static equilibrium model if the system can never reach an equilibrium or if the equilibrium is unstable.

Rose-Ackerman's (1979) model is similar to Westhoff's except that there are absentee landlords, and taxes in each town are flat-rate property taxes. There are a fixed number of towns, each town has a fixed land area, and residents consume land rather than housing. Thus, this model is at almost the opposite extreme from Hamilton's where housing supply is perfectly elastic and communities enter freely. In Rose-Ackerman, landowners have no political power but the supply of land to each town is completely inelastic. Therefore, each towns' tax base may be different, and this fact can influence voters' choices. The equilibrium, if one exists, will reflect the accidents of geography and boundary definition as well as differences in underlying tastes.

Citizens have utility functions defined over free income, land, and public services. In a fully general model with three arguments in the utility function, voting cycles are likely so that the majority rule does not produce determinate

---

[12]*This is formally demonstrated in Westhoff (1977). See also Brueckner (1979). Beliveau (1981) has extended Westhoff's model to incude a linear income tax system of the form $t_i(y) = a_i + b_i y(n)$, where a_i and b_i are parameters chosen by citizens of community i and $y(n)$ is the income of the nth citizen. She shows that such a tax system is incompatible with equilibrium.*

results.[13] Thus, Rose-Ackerman makes very strong assumptions about tastes and information to prevent cycles. She expresses voters' utility "indirectly" as a function of public services, land prices, and free income. Given a property tax on land, her strongest assumption is that people can be ranked unambiguously in terms of their preferences for public services versus land prices irrespective of the level of free income. This "separability" condition means that majority rule within a town will produce a unique choice in each referendum. Voters are as myopic in this model as in Westhoff's. They do not take account of the migration produced by public choices, and when they migrate they are similarly myopic--each town's mixture of public services and land rents is taken as given. Given a fixed number of towns, each with a fixed land area, Rose-Ackerman shows that, even with voting cycles assumed away and no wealth effects, neither existence nor stability of equilibrium is assured. Even if an equilibrium does exist, it is unlikely to be efficient because the result is determined in part by each community's fixed land area.[14]

In both Westhoff and Rose-Ackerman, people are very myopic. When they vote, they do not anticipate any in or out migration, and when they migrate, they assume that public service levels and tax rates will remain constant. No one has examined the way changed information assumptions would change the results of such majority rule models. The only paper I have found that contrasts myopic with farsighted behavior is by Stiglitz (1977). Unfortunately, he only carries out this contrast for the case where everyone is alike and each community has the same amount of land. He develops a general equilibrium model where land is an input in the production of both private and public goods. In each community, governments must decide how much labor to use producing public versus private goods. Migration thus shifts production opportunities. When voters do not own land and do not anticipate the migration induced by public choices, then there are Pareto inferior equilibria that are stable and Pareto

[13]*Single-peakedness essentially requires that the public choice can be reduced to a choice over the level of a single variable. Thus, any multi-dimensional choice problem is likely to produce voting cycles. See Feldman (1980).*
[14]*See also Bewley (1981) and Pauly (1976) for similar results using somewhat different models. In contrast, Epple, Filimon, and Romer (1981) show that an equilibrium will exist in a similar model where the local public good is subject to crowding. This assumption, of course, counteracts the tax base benefits provided by immigration (see also Stiglitz, 1977, and in this volume.)*

efficient equilibria may be unstable. When people are not "myopic," they choose their community's level of public services by assuming that the other town will hold public services constant and calculating the migration that will occur. Under these conditions, an equilibrium with equal-sized communities is stable. It is not obvious, however, that Stiglitz's identical-individual model has much relevance for the case of heterogeneous individuals. Indeed, although Stiglitz discusses models with heterogeneous individuals later in his paper, he does not return to the contrast between myopic and farsighted voters. The more general case is more difficult because entrants affect both the resource or tax base, *and* the community's mixture of tastes. Voters, however, do not seem to have always recognized this latter possibility.[15] Some communities, for example, have permitted the development of housing for the elderly only to discover that the new childless residents vote against school tax referenda.

C. Capital Gains and Politics

There has been considerable discussion among economists about whether interjurisdictional political differences are capitalized into property values. If people vary in tastes and incomes, then observed price differences will not reflect anyone's relative valuation of different communities. With no zoning, the actual pattern of prices is the envelope of the bid-rent lines of different groups in the population with each town occupied by people willing to bid the most for it. Thus, differences in public services and taxes will be reflected in property values, but prices will not be set so that everyone is indifferent to his or her location. Voters who own property will have an incentive to choose public ser-

[15]*If newspapers reports are to be believed, a striking example of this phenomenon occurred in Ft. Lee, New Jersey. This community, across the George Washington Bridge from New York City, was long known as a gambling haven. Apparently, many underworld figures used gambling profits to purchase property there and, given a sympathetic town government, they built high-rise apartment houses. These apartments were soon inhabited by middle-class tenants who voted the old politicians out of office and tried to eliminate corruption and underworld infuence from the town (*New York Times, September 10, 11, 1974*)*.

vice levels that raise property values, but housing price differentials are not an accurate measure of the net benefits of government services.

If, however, one taste class is the sole occupant of more than one town, then relative price differences between these towns will reflect that group's relative valuation of public services versus housing. Even here, though, one cannot measure the net benefits of public services by looking only at the variation in unit housing prices, since presumably people will purchase more housing in the low-priced town than in the high-priced town. Price differences will exactly measure benefits only if the demand for housing is perfectly inelastic.

Those who deny the importance of capitalization have not been concerned with these difficulties. They have, instead, emphasized the supply side of the market. They point out that if one town has high property values, builders will concentrate activity there, new towns will enter, and other towns will change their policies to emulate the high value communities. All of these possibilities push the competitive analogy too far. First, although many towns have some vacant land, the supply of housing in most towns cannot realistically be described as infinitely elastic. Second, the entry of new towns managed by developers is a costly undertaking. Finally, towns will seek to copy high property value towns only if residents are only interested in capital gains. However, renters view high property values as a cost rather than a benefit, and even owners will not care only about capital gains if moving is costly or if they wish to purchase additional housing in the community.

Taken together, a realistic view of the housing market suggests that capital gains are possible but that they are not the only things that matter to voters. Incorporating capital gains into a more general local government model is difficult for two reasons. First, it is no longer possible to assume that voters are myopic. By definition, a person who anticipates capital gains must try to predict the future demand for residential property and in a world of varied tastes and incomes, voters may also try to predict the political preferences of immigrants. Second, if voters care both about capital gains and about tax and spending levels *per se*, majority rule may not give determinate results since preferences need not be single-peaked. In addition, housing price increases may be seen as both benefits and costs. Increases raise a homeowner's wealth but make it more costly to buy a larger house in the community.

Beyond Tiebout

These difficulties have so far prevented the development of a general model with capital gains.[16] Yinger (forthcoming), however, has made a preliminary attempt. His results parallel the work of Bewley (1981) and Stiglitz (1977) since he also shows that a Tiebout world is likely to be inefficient. Capitalization is not eliminated in the long run because of the opportunity cost of land, and "local voting cannot eliminate distortions in the housing market due to the property tax." Nevertheless, Yinger's research is limited by the model he uses. He assumes that a stable long-run equilibrium exists and then examines the characteristics of that equilibrium. However, as the simpler models of Rose-Ackerman (1977) and Westhoff (1977, 1979) show, stable equilibria may not exist in models that seek to combine political and market behavior. Furthermore, Yinger's modeling tactic makes the problem tractable at the expense of many of the most interesting issues that arise in discussions of capitalization. Thus, capital gains play no independent role because in long-run equilibrium these gains do not affect voters' marginal choices of tax and spending levels. In addition, voters gain nothing from trying to predict the public choices of new entrants since when the system is in equilibrium, movers have no impact on political decisions. In a heterogeneous community this means that "the people bidding on the median voter's house have the same preferences as the median voter" --a strong and not very plausible condition. In short, Yinger's long-run equilibrium assumption means that his model is not as different from models with absentee ownership as it might at first appear. While Yinger has taken a first step, we clearly need to find better ways to model the wealth effects of public choices.

D. *Monopoly Models of Local Government*

The final group of political models assumes that a single group or individual controls each town's political choices. In these models, the normative justification for a multiple government system is typically very different from Tiebout's. Decentralization is seen not as a way to take account of heterogeneity in tastes, but as a way to avoid the costs of monopoly control. However, as Epple and Zelenitz (1981) show, once the land market is taken into account, decentrali-

---

[16]*Starrett's recent work (1981) on capitalization is not an exception since he entirely ignores politics. Instead, he simply assumes that a change in the level of public good provision occurs, and then considers how land and housing values will be affected.*

zation will not eliminate the "profits" of government officials so long as it is costly for old communities to expand or for new communities to enter the "market." In their admittedly extreme model--where politicians maximize the excess of revenues over expenditures and all households are alike--the possibility of migration does not eliminate all "profit" both because each community has limited space, and because new entrants are constrained to choose less desirable locations.

Sonstelie and Portney (1978), in contrast, argue in favor of another kind of monopoly power. They claim that efficiency will be guaranteed if each town maximizes aggregate property values, and they go on to recommend compensation schemes that could produce this result. Along with White (1975), they show that it will be inefficient for owners of developed land to seek to maximize their wealth by controlling the development of vacant land. Thus, Sonstelie and Portney propose that owners of undeveloped land be compensated for growth restrictions. However, before one goes too far to "fine-tune" such a system, it is well to take account of Brueckner's (1980) critique. He shows that Sonstelie and Portney's result depends upon their failure to specify equilibrium conditions in the housing market. Brueckner shows that each individual community would be efficient with a "house tax" (i.e., a head tax on each homeowner) if one holds conditions elsewhere fixed. However, competitive property value maximization need not generate a globally efficient equilibrium because the allocation of people among communities may be inefficient.[17]

All of these monopoly models are limited by a failure to specify the way monopolists manage to acquire and maintain power. One wonders why mayoral candidates don't run against "profit-maximizing" incumbents in Epple and Zelenitz's model, or how a cartel of property owners can be maintained if the relative gain to each owner varies as public policy varies. Even if compensation is possible, it might be worthwhile for a majority to leave the cartel and pass laws that favor them

---

[17] *See also the similar but somewhat more general results in Starrett (1980). Starrett ignores the problems of local public choice and assumes that each community is controlled by a planner who maximizes a welfare function that depends upon the utility of the town's initial resident-property owners. This is close to a property value maximization assumption except that other influences on welfare are also considered. He shows that communities may over- or under-expand depending upon the nature of taxation.*

at the expense of the rest of the community. Coalition formation and bargaining strength must be incorporated into the discussion.

IV. TOWARD A POLITICAL ECONOMY OF LOCAL GOVERNMENT

A. *Normative Issues*

Existing research on the political economy of local government has two major failings—one normative and the other positive. On the one hand, the models neglect distributive issues that are an important part of the normative argument against "fragmented" local government. On the other hand, monopoly models seem very inadequate as a descriptive matter, and majority rule models, although a useful beginning, cannot be expanded to incorporate realistic complexities.

Turning to the normative issue first, the fragmentation of metropolitan government systems has frequently been criticized because it permits wealthy people to cluster together and avoid paying taxes that provide benefits to low income people. A multiple government system is clearly not well-suited to carrying out distributive goals. Thus, students of federalism (*e.g.*, Oates, 1972) argue in favor of placing redistributive programs at higher levels of government. If this were done, then the clustering of people by income would be no more reprehensible than the tendency of the rich to purchase new luxury cars while the poor buy used cars.

We ought, however, to assess the benefits of multiple government systems not only in a first-best world but also in a realistic second-best world where public services such as education are financed, in part, by local governments. In many states, policy has been directed toward reducing interjurisdictional differences in tax base per pupil (see Rubinfeld, 1979). To some extent, these tax base differences are caused by differences in the non-residential property tax base, but part of the difference is due to residential property. A person committed to using willingness-to-pay as a criterion for public service provision would want to eliminate the former differences but not the latter. Yet, the quality of education does have implications for the distribution of income across generations. Permitting the wealthy to purchase better education for their children than the poor can afford is likely to give wealthy children a long-run advantage over poor children.

Some services, however, are less redistributive in character and, therefore, the Tiebout mechanism has more normative appeal. Here the problem is the lack of effective options for many low income people. Existing models assume costless migration in a world where local public service differences are the main determinant of household location choices. In fact, residential choices are also influenced by job locations and by the characteristics of the housing stock at each location. Therefore, one important historical fact--the existence of a single central city, much larger than the suburbs and containing a concentration of jobs and old housing--will have a major impact on the operational significance of local government models. Within this structure, low income people are likely to have few effective local government choices. The actual choices that poor people make, even if moving is costless, may be largely determined by accessibility and the housing stock, not by public service levels. Thus, the existence of a central city is bound up with a discussion of the welfare effects of a multiple government system (see Rothenberg, 1976; Bradford and Oates, 1974; White, 1975). If the quality and cost of public services is determined by the demographic characteristics of the population (see Oates, 1981), then the poor's limited ability to outbid the rich for desirable residential locations can raise the cost of public services for poor families. If these effects are important, then a multiple government system cannot be evaluated as if it led to the efficient provision of services, and low income people may be worse off in a multiple government region than in one with a metropolitan government (see Burstein, 1980).[18]

B. Positive Issues

Positive political-economic models of local government should not assume either costless migration, perfect sorting, or a simple relationship between citizens' tastes and public choices. Existing evidence indicates that in spite of average income differences between communities, intracommunity variation in income is typically very large (see Pack and Pack, 1977, 1978). Although the central cities' concentration of jobs and old housing draws many low income people to that location, other communities also have some poor housing

[18]*These cautions do not mean that a single metropolitan government is necessarily desirable. Some people do apparently benefit from the variety produced by a multiple government system (see Bradford and Oates, 1974) and poor people would be likely to have even less voting power in a metropolitan government than in a fragmented system (see Banfield, 1957).*

and some low-skilled jobs nearby. The large size of the central city combined with its concentration of jobs, shops, and leisure activities assures that its population will be heterogeneous and that many people will have few realistic options. In the suburbs, so long as zoning laws are not perfectly effective, some low income people may choose to live near some wealthy people even if the poor have a very low willingness-to-pay for public services. Although integration by income levels may, in part, occur because of the external benefits to the poor of living in a mixed-income community, other important reasons are the cost of moving and the locational and housing characteristics of various towns.

More generally, urban housing markets operate with many frictions because of the durability of housing, the costs of moving and the importance of neighborhood effects. Therefore, a city is unlikely to be in long-run equilibrium at any particular point in time. The pattern of household location reflects both the relatively permanent locational characteristics of various sites *and* the fact that it is costly to adjust to long-run equilibrium. Furthermore, the political system in most towns also operates with frictions. Changes in government behavior may not closely track changes in people's tastes or opportunities because elections are scheduled infrequently or elected representatives control information and set agendas for the populace.

This means that the most pressing research task is the development of more sophisticated models of local government. Much empirical work in this area has too uncritically accepted median voter models or monopoly models which assume the governments maximize "economic welfare." As the theoretical work emphasizes, median voter models only apply if one is willing to make very strong assumptions about either the choices available or the tastes of residents. Conversely, monopoly power models assume either a remarkable similarity of interest among voters or a single dominant coalition that controls government. These empirical assertions must be documented before strong claims could be made for either view.

In general, it will not be fruitful to seek *the* objective function for government to maximize. Monopoly power models will not usually be sufficient as descriptions of reality. Models of this kind have been developed by both economists and sociologists. Economists have emphasized the monopoly power of property owners or public officials while sociologists have stressed the dominance of a small high-status elite. Although their methods of modeling and of doing empirical research are very different, these two types of research have one thing in common--in both cases, the research fails to explain how such monopoly power could be exercised and maintained (for a critique of the sociological research, see Polsby, 1980).

Similarly, simple majority rule models also are not sufficient. Yet, much empirical work by economists on the demand for public services works with an oversimplified version of the median voter model. Neglecting the possibilities of both strategic behavior and of intercommunity migration, this research supposes that community decisions will reflect the preferences of people with the town's median income. The discussion of these models frequently neglects the possibility that the person with the median income need not be the median voter, and that, in fact, no median voter need exist. Nevertheless, empirical work has found positive income elasticities although the range of values is wide (see Inman, 1979). The range in the results suggests not only the inadequacy of the data but also the weakness of the underlying model of politics. (For a critique of this research, see Romer and Rosenthal, 1979.) Something else besides a community's median income appears to be instrumental in determining the results.

Most politicans would not, of course, disagree with the observation that simple majority rule models are inadequate. Studies of legislative behavior (see Fenno, 1966; Shick, 1980) indicate that elected representatives understand well the importance of agenda manipulation and strategic behavior.[19] Real political life, moreover, takes place in real time and this is an important constraint on behavior. Compromises are forced by the fact that political decisions must be reached within a particular time limit. Conflict is diffused both by decentralizing the choice process so no one can see the whole package and by raising only incremental choices. Thus, it is not an argument against the results of public choice theory to point out that voting cycles "never occur." Instead, one might suppose that intransitivity is very prevalent given the redistributive nature of public spending programs, but that political systems are organized to prevent these disagreements from bringing government to a halt.

[19]*Recent theoretical work by Gibbard (1973) and Satterthwaite (1975) demonstrates the pervasiveness of strategic behavior in theoretical models of public choice. They impose a set of weak conditions and show that if one wishes to associate a single social choice with each pattern of individual preferences, then the process will not be cheat-proof. Cheat-proofness or non-manipulability means that no one finds it in his interest to misrepresent his preferences to gain an advantage. See Feldman (1980, pp. 196-215).*

Therefore, it would seem useful to develop a political-economic approach that looks at the way a multiple government system affects the bargaining power of various groups in the population. The theoretical development of such models can be viewed as an extension of a research approach that stresses the importance of politics *per se*, examines the centralization or decentralization of power, and tries to explain why a person or group is powerful in one context and not in another (e.g., Banfield, 1961; Dahl, 1961; Banfield and Wilson, 1963; Wolfinger, 1974; Ziegler, Jennings, and Peak, 1974; Polsby, 1980). Surprisingly, this branch of political science seldom mentions exit possibilities as a source of power (for a general discussion of "exit" and "voice," see Hirshman, 1970). There is a sense, then, in which work on city politics has not captured an essential feature of local government. If one takes account of the differential costs of moving to another jurisdiction, this information might illuminate some otherwise puzzling features of local government. For example, very poorly organized groups might have considerable influence over some decisions simply because they can exit easily and because they are valuable to the rest of the population. A central city may try to retain wealthy households and existing employers because they contribute to the city's tax base (see Peterson, 1979). These groups may not need to engage in any organized or explicit political action at all. So long as they can inexpensively leave the community, this possibility constrains the rest of the population.

In contrast, other groups are vulnerable to "exploitation" because their own prosperity and livelihood are closely tied to a particular jurisdiction. As a consequence, they have a particularly strong incentive to organize politically. Thus, local retailers and bankers have an incentive to be involved in local politics because their prosperity depends on the town's economic health (see Margolis, 1974; Sayre and Kaufman, 1960). Here the differential organizing ability of various groups will be important. They must overcome free rider problems that do not arise for those who can simply leave town.

One group with a large stock in local government is public employees themselves, and this is one area where some progress has been made in modeling behavior. Romer and Rosenthal (1978) show how government bureaucrats can use their power to set agendas as a means of increasing budgetary size even when decisions are made by majority vote. In recent extensions, they have sought to take account of the imperfect information available to both government officials and voters, and have begun empirical tests (see Romer and Rosenthal in this volume and the papers cited therein).

Crecine (1970) assumes that public officials want a quiet life with few conflicts and thus use rigid, incremental procedures to set budgets. Especially interesting is the work of Courant, Gramlich, and Rubinfeld (1979) and Gramlich and Rubinfeld (1980). They model public employees' attempts to obtain high wages and high levels of public output and show how their behavior is constrained by the migration possibilities of privately employed workers.

Local governments are constrained not only by the exit possibilities of citizens and business interests, but also by the federal structure of government. More work needs to be done which integrates the study of local government with the study of federalism--since the possibility of raising issues at the state or national level constrains the behavior of local politicans. Most economic work on federalism has been normative (*e.g.*, Oates, 1972) and depicts higher levels of government as taking over tasks that create interjurisdictional externalities in metropolitan regions. Higher levels would regulate or subsidize lower levels to induce them to produce efficiently. However, we also need a positive analysis of the strategic possibilities of federalism. Work in political science, however, has been generally rather atheoretical (for a literature review, see Riker, 1975), but the area appers to be a fruitful one for future research (for one preliminary attempt, see Rose-Ackerman, 1980, 1981).

These are promising beginnings that point toward a political-economic theory of local government, but we need richer analytical models that can build on past work on multigovernment systems and incorporate at least some of the insights of political scientists' studies of government. It seems likely that such a broad interdisciplinary perspective can, in time, lead to real progress in understanding the way metropolitan areas are governed.

REFERENCES

Arrow, K. J., 1951. *Social Choice and Individual Values*. New York: Wiley, (rev. ed., 1963).

Banfield, E., 1957. "The Politics of Metropolitan Area Organization," *Midwest Journal of Political Science* 1:77-91.

Banfield, E., 1961. *Political Influence*. New York: The Free Press.

Banfield, E., and J. Q. Wilson, 1963. *City Politics*. Cambridge: Harvard University Press.

Beliveau, B., 1981. "Two Aspects of Market Signaling," unpublished Ph.D. Dissertation, Yale University.

Bewley, T., 1981. "A Critique of Tiebout's Theory of Local Public Expenditures," *Econometrica* 49:713-740.

Bradford, D. F., and W. E. Oates, 1974. "Suburban Exploitation of Central Cities and Government Structure," in H. M. Hochman and G. E. Peterson (eds.) *Redistribution Through Public Choice.* New York: Columbia University Press.

Brainard, W. C., and T. Dolbear, 1967. "The Possibility of Oversupply of Local Public Goods," *Journal of Political Economy* 75:86-92.

Brueckner, J. K., 1979. "Equilibrium in a System of Communities with Local Public Goods: A Diagrammatic Exposition," *Economic Letters* 2:387-393.

Brueckner, J. K., 1980. "Property Value Maximization and Public Sector Efficiency," University of Illinois at Urbana Working Paper.

Brueckner, J. K., 1981. "Zoning and Property Taxation in a System of Local Governments: Further Analysis," *Urban Studies* 18:113-121.

Buchanan, J. M., and C. J. Goetz, 1972. "Efficiency Limits of Fiscal Mobility: An Assessment of the Tiebout Model," *Journal of Public Economics* 1:25-44.

Burstein, N., 1980. "Voluntary Income Clustering and the Demand for Housing and Local Public Goods," *Journal of Urban Economics* 7:175-185.

Courant, P. N., E. M. Gramlich, and D. L. Rubinfeld, 1979. "Public Employee Market Power and the Level of Government Spending," *American Economic Review* 69:806-817.

Crecine, J. P. (ed.), 1970. *Financing the Metropolis.* Beverly Hills, California: Sage.

Dahl, R., 1961. *Who Governs?* New Haven: Yale University Press.

Edel, M. D., and E. D. Sclar, 1974. "Taxes, Spending, and Property Values: Supply Adjustment in a Tiebout-Oates Model," *Journal of Political Economy* 82:941-954.

Ellickson, B., 1979a. "Competitive Equilibrium in Local Public Goods," *Journal of Economic Theory* 21:46-61.

Ellickson, B., 1979b. "Local Public Goods and the Market for Neighborhoods," in D. Segal (ed.). *The Economics of Neighborhood.* New York: Academic Press.

Epple, D., and A. Zelenitz, 1981. "The Implications of Competition Among Jurisdictions: Does Tiebout Need Politics?", *Journal of Political Economy* 89:1197-1217.

Epple, D., R. Filimon, and T. Romer, 1981. "Housing, Voting, and Moving: Equilibrium in a Model of Local Public Goods with Multiple Jurisdictions," Carnegie-Mellon University Working Paper.

Feldman, A. M., 1980. *Welfare Economics and Social Choice Theory*. Boston: Martinus Nijhoff.
Fenno, R., 1966. *The Power of the Purse: Appropriations Politics in Congress*. Boston: Little, Brown.
Flatters, F., J. V. Henderson, and P. M. Mieszkowski, 1974. "Public Goods, Efficiency, and Regional Equalization," *Journal of Public Economics* 3:99-112.
Gibbard, A., 1973. "Manipulation of Voting Schemes: A General Result," *Econometrica* 41:587-602.
Gramlich, E. M., and D. L. Rubinfeld, 1980. "Public Employment, Voting, and Spending Tastes: Some Empirical Evidence," University of Michigan Discussion Paper No. 156.
Hamilton, B. W., 1975. "Zoning and Property Taxation in a System of Local Governments," *Urban Studies* 12:205-211.
Hamilton, B. W., 1976. "Capitalization of Intrajurisdictional Differences in Local Tax Prices," *American Economic Review* 66:743-753.
Hirschman, A. O., 1970. *Exit, Voice and Loyalty*. Cambridge: Harvard University Press.
Inman, R. P., 1979. "The Fiscal Performance of Local Governments: An Interpretative Review," in P. Mieszkowski and M. Straszheim (eds.), *Current Issues in Urban Economics*. Baltimore: Johns Hopkins University Press.
Kramer, G. H., 1973. "On a Class of Equilibrium Conditions for Majority Rule," *Econometrica* 41:285-297.
Margolis, J., 1955. "A Comment on the Pure Theory of Public Expenditure," *Review of Economics and Statistics* 37:247-249.
Margolis, J., 1974. "Public Policies for Private Profits: Urban Government," in H. M. Hochman and G. E. Peterson (eds.), *Redistribution Through Public Choice*. New York: Columbia University Press.
McGuire, M. C., 1974. "Group Segregation and Optimal Jurisdictions," *Journal of Political Economy* 82:112-132.
Musgrave, R. A., 1959. *Theory of Public Finance*. New York: McGraw Hill.
Oates, W. E., 1972. *Fiscal Federalism*. New York: Harcourt Brace, Jovanovich.
Oates, W. E., 1981. "On Local Finance and the Tiebout Model," *American Economic Review (Papers and Proceedings)* 71:93-98.
Pack, H., and J. R. Pack, 1977. "Metropolitan Fragmentation and Suburban Homogeneity," *Urban Studies* 14:191-201.
Pack, H., and J. R. Pack, 1978. "Metropolitan Fragmentation and Local Public Expenditures," *National Tax Journal* 31:349-362.

Pauly, M. V., 1976. "A Model of Local Government Expenditure and Tax Capitalization," *Journal of Public Economics* 6: 231-242.
Pestieau, P., 1980. "Fiscal Mobility and Local Public Goods: A Survey of the Empirical and Theoretical Studies of the Tiebout Model," Université Catholique de Louvain, Louvain-la-Neuve, Belgium, Research Program: Spatial Analysis and Public Services Policy, Paper No. 6.
Peterson, P., 1979. "A Unitary Model of Local Taxation and Expenditure Policies in the United States," *British Journal of Political Science* 9:281-314.
Polsby, N., 1980. *Community Power and Political Theory*. New Haven: Yale University Press.
Richter, D. K., forthcoming. "Weakly Democratic Regular Tax Equilibria in a Local Public Goods Economy with Perfect Consumer Mobility," *Journal of Economic Theory*.
Riker, W. H., 1975. "Federalism," in F. Greenstein and N. Polsby (eds.), *Governmental Institutions and Processes*. Reading, Mass.: Addison-Wesley.
Romer, T., and H. Rosenthal, 1978. "Bureaucrats vs. Voters: On the Political Economy of Resource Allocation by Direct Democracy," *Public Choice* 33:27-43.
Romer, T., and H. Rosenthal, 1979. "The Elusive Median Voter," *Journal of Public Economics* 12:143-170.
Romer, T., and H. Rosenthal, 1982. "Voting and Spending: Some Empirical Relationships in the Political Economy of Local Public Finance," Chapter 8 of this volume.
Rose-Ackerman, S., 1977. "On the Distribution of Public Program Benefits Between Landlords and Tenants," *Journal of Environmental Economics and Management* 4:150-170.
Rose-Ackerman, S., 1979. "Market Models of Local Government: Exit, Voting, and the Land Market," *Journal of Urban Economics* 6:319-337.
Rose-Ackerman, S., 1980. "Risktaking and Reelection: Does Federalism Promote Innovation?" *Journal of Legal Studies* 9:593-616.
Rose-Ackerman, S., 1981. "Does Federalism Matter: Political Choice in a Federal Republic," *Journal of Political Economy* 89:152-165.
Rothenberg, J., 1976. "Endogenous City-Suburb Governmental Rivalry Through Household Location," in W. E. Oates (ed.), *The Political Economy of Multi-Level Government*. Lexington, Mass.: D. C. Heath.
Rubinfeld, D. L., 1979. "Judicial Approaches to Local Public-Sector Equity: An Economic Analysis," in P. Mieszkowski and M. Straszheim (eds.), *Current Issues in Urban Economics*. Baltimore: Johns Hopkins University Press.

Samuelson, P. A., 1954. "The Pure Theory of Public Expenditures," *Review of Economics and Statistics* 36:387-389.

Sandler, T., and J. T. Tschirhart, 1980. "The Economic Theory of Clubs: An Evaluative Survey," *Journal of Economic Literature* 18:1481-1521.

Satterthwaite, M. A., 1975. "Strategy-Proofness and Arrow's Conditions: Existence and Correspondence Theorems for Voting Procedures and Social Welfare Functions," *Journal of Economic Theory* 10:187-217.

Sayre, W. W., and H. Kaufman, 1960. *Governing New York City.* New York: Russell Sage Foundation.

Shick, A., 1980. *Congress and Money.* Washington: The Urban Institute.

Sonstelie, J. C., and P. R. Portney, 1978. "Profit Maximizing Communities and the Theory of Local Public Expenditures," *Journal of Urban Economics* 5:263-277.

Starrett, D. A., 1980. "On the Method of Taxation and the Provision of Local Public Goods," *American Economic Review* 70:380-392.

Starrett, D. A., 1981. "Land Value Capitalization in Local Public Finance," *Journal of Political Economy* 89:306-327.

Stiglitz, J. E., 1977. "The Theory of Local Public Goods," in M. S. Feldstein and R. F. Inman (eds.), *The Economics of Public Services.* London: Macmillan.

Stiglitz, J. E., 1982. "The Theory of Public Goods Twenty-Five Years After Tiebout: A Perspective," Chapter 2 of this volume.

Tiebout, C. M., 1956. "A Pure Theory of Local Expenditures," *Journal of Political Economy* 64:416-424.

Westhoff, F. H., 1977. "Existence of Equilibria in Economies with a Local Public Good," *Journal of Economic Theory* 14:84-112.

Westhoff, F. H., 1979. "Policy Inferences from Community Choice Models: A Caution," *Journal of Urban Economics* 6:535-549.

Wheaton, W. C., 1975. "Consumer Mobility and Community Tax Bases: The Financing of Local Public Goods," *Journal of Public Economics* 4:377-384.

White, M. J., 1975. "Fiscal Zoning in Fragmented Metropolitan Areas," in E. S. Mills and W. E. Oates (eds.), *Fiscal Zoning and Land Use Control.* Lexington, Mass.: D. C. Heath.

Williams, A., 1966. "The Optimal Provision of Public Goods in a System of Local Governments," *Journal of Political Economy* 74:18-33.

Wolfinger, R. E., 1974. *The Politics of Progress.* Englewood Cliffs, N.J.: Prentice-Hall.

Yinger, J., forthcoming. "Capitalization and the Theory of Local Public Finance," *Journal of Political Economy*.

Ziegler, L. H., M. K. Jennings, and G. W. Peak, 1974. *Governing American Schools: Political Interaction in Local School Districts*. N. Scituate, Mass.: Duxbury Press.

Chapter 4

A REVIEW: IS THE PROPERTY TAX A BENEFIT TAX?

Bruce W. Hamilton

Department of Political Economy
The Johns Hopkins University
Baltimore, Maryland

I. INTRODUCTION

Is the property tax a benefit tax? Or, to ask the same question differently, does the delivery system for locally provided public services have the same efficiency and distribution properties as a system of undistorted markets? Assuming no distortions in the rest of the economy, this question can be further refined to: Do local governments offer bundles of services which are produced in a technically efficient manner, and do consumers receive the quantities which they would have demanded in a market delivery system? As this taxonomy suggests, a useful way to examine the original question is to consider separately the supply and demand of local public services. Section II lays out the Tiebout "orthodoxy" (that the property tax is a benefit tax) in its modern form, subdivided into considerations of demand and supply. Section III is a consideration of both orthodox and New Right (Leviathan) challenges to the Tiebout orthodoxy.

My reading of the theoretical and empirical literature leads me to believe that the Tiebout mechanism does provide some force toward efficiency (and toward no redistribution). But surely more explicit market mechanisms would yield substantial efficiency benefits with few additional costs.

II. THE TIEBOUT ORTHODOXY

A. Demand

Tiebout's (1956) paper, and much of the literature which directly follows from it, is basically demand oriented, with but fleeting reference to production. The Tiebout foot-voting mechanism is a demanders' response mechanism, a means whereby households assign themselves to the various public service offerings according to demand. Indeed, a major purpose of Tiebout's paper is to note that the possibility of foot-voting provides a mechanism whereby it is rational for consumers to reveal their preferences for public services.

The original Tiebout model is an incomplete statement of the demand side of the public-service market in that it does not fully spell out the structure of prices faced by consumers. And only when we know that consumers face efficient prices do we know that they will make efficient marketplace decisions. My favorite statement of this pricing mechanism is Hamilton (1976a), but there are other important contributions, which I will touch upon. A summary statement of this theoretical work is that there is a tendency toward efficient pricing, though the sets of assumptions which necessarily yield perfection in the pricing mechanism strain credulity (see Hamilton, 1975;[1] Portney and Sonstelie, 1980).

1. Capitalization.[2] The property tax might be converted into an efficient price via capitalization--the mechanism whereby property values vary to reflect variations in taxes and public-sector benefits. Consumers will be faced with an efficient set of price signals if, for all houses,

$$V + T = C(H) + C(LPS). \tag{1}$$

---

[1] *In this model, capitalization is not considered and free migration forces an equilibrium in which all houses in a jurisdiction are of equal value. In the 1976a paper, all of the interesting economic properties remain even though house values (and utility functions) vary within jurisdictions. Many researchers (see Rose-Ackerman in this volume) have missed this relaxation of the perfect segregation result, thus thinking that the efficiency story is more restrictive than it really is.*

[2] *My discussion of capitalization is fairly terse, with only enough detail to establish the relationship between capitalization and pricing. For a fuller description of both theory and empirical evidence, see Bloom, Ladd, and Yinger in this volume.*

In words, house value, V, plus property taxes, T, must be equal to the opportunity cost of the resources devoted to providing the housing service, $C(H)$, plus the average (equal to marginal) cost of providing the public services, $C(LPS)$. If this equality prevails throughout the spectrum of offerings, every bundle of housing services plus local public services costs what it would if the public services were offered explicitly for an average-cost price. Thus the household's budget constraint is what it would be under a user-charge system (except for the possibility of unavailable bundles), and an efficient outcome will emerge from consumers' private decisions.[3]

Generally we refer to the above case as complete capitalization--any deviation of $C(LPS)$ from T is exactly offset by a reverse deviation of V from $C(H)$. Within a jurisdiction (assuming identical public-service deliveries to all households) complete capitalization implies that property values deviate from housing-resource cost by an amount equal to the property's tax deviation from the jurisdiction mean. A property the prevalue of whose taxes are $5000 below the mean will command $5000 more when sold than is warranted by the cost of the attached resources.

The empirical implications of (1) across jurisdictions are slightly different. In a world with no intergovernmental transfers and no non-residential property, all capitalization effects within a jurisdiction will wash (see Hamilton, 1976a), with the result that mean property value in each jurisdiction will be just equal to the cost of the house resources. If we think of (1) as a regression, and if the observations are jurisdiction means, (moving T to the right-hand side) $C(H)$ will explain the entire variance in V, and T and $C(LPS)$ (which will be identical to one another, except for sign) will have no effect. This observation has unfortunately led some observers (see Hamilton, 1975) to refer to this case as zero capitalization rather than full capitalization, thus creating some confusion in the literature.

The above discussion contains no behavioral modeling--it merely states the empirical conditions under which consumers face an efficient price vector. Our next task is to examine the theory to see whether we can expect such an outcome to occur, and our subsequent task will be to examine the empirical literature.

[3]*The equivalence of efficient pricing and 100% capitalization can be demonstrated by showing that 100% capitalization (and complete offerings) leaves the household with the same budget constraint as under a regime with no taxes and average cost prices for local public services.*

2. *Theory*. Except for the case where property taxes are the only source of local revenue and each jurisdiction is perfectly homogeneous, capitalization requires that the values of some houses deviate from the cost of the resources required to provide the housing. In an uninhibited housing-construction market, these property-value deviations will be driven away by supply adjustment.[4] But in the Tiebout world, producers are not the only agents who wish to influence the stocks of various types of housing. If a jurisdiction permits construction of fiscally-advantaged housing, fiscal disadvantage will be imposed upon the pre-existing housing stock, and this will lead to capital losses. So existing residents (the electorate) will always oppose the construction of fiscally-advantaged housing, so as to protect the capital values of their homes.[5] The outcome of this disagreement over construction depends upon the relative strengths of developers and the local government's land-use controls. In addition, the outcome determines the degree of capitalization. The range of possibilities is from zero to more than 100% capitalization (in the first case suppliers eliminate all deviations of property values from resource costs, and in the latter fiscally advantaged housing is so severely restricted that it commands a value above the sum of resource cost and fiscal advantage).

[4]*It is not clear that such an equilibrium is stable. Supply equilibrium requires that all property values be equal (after correcting for size of house), and demand equilibrium requires horizontal equality. As nearly as I have been able to tell, these conditions hold simultaneously only in the case where all jurisdictions have the same mix of housing qualities. But regardless of this, the basic point in the text remains: Suppliers will want to expand the stock of low-income housing as compared with the full-capitalization outcome.*

[5]*It is possible but implausible that restriction will be superfluous--that households will voluntarily sort themselves into segregated jurisdictions (see Ellickson, 1971). This will occur if demand for public services is quite income elastic (so that a rich jurisdiction's offering of public services is a long way off the poor person's demand curve) and the demand for housing is income inelastic (this will cause the poor person's tax subsidy to be rather small). In fact, the demand for housing appears to be more elastic (approximately 1.0, see deLeeuw, 1971) than that for public services (around 0.7, see Bergstrom and Goodman, 1973). Also, land zoned for low-income housing frequently sells for as much as two or three times otherwise identical non-zoned land, strongly suggesting involuntary segregation.*

To my knowledge, there are only three mechanisms which would ensure an efficient outcome (100% capitalization). The first is a well-greased system of bribes (paid by developers to the local treasury, not to the zoning officials). So long as the bribe exceeds the tax-revenue loss associated with construction of low-income housing, the government will grant zoning variances. And up to the point at which the bribe which can be profitably offered covers the lost taxes, efficiency is enhanced by expanding the supply of low-income housing. Indeed, in many jurisdictions such a system exists to some degree. The bribes are generally offered in-kind, with the developer offering to provide streets, storm drainage, parkland, and so on, in exchange for permission to build.

The second is a law of zoning with compensation. (This is a special case of the system of bribes described above.) Here the mechanism for bribes is straightforward; efficiency requires only that the compensation to current owners for rezoning be set equal to the present value of the revenue loss.

The third mechanism which would ensure an efficient outcome is total land value maximization as the objective of the local government. If the government pursues this goal rather than that of maximization of the per-household tax base, then it will pursue an efficient land management policy (see Portney and Sonstelie, 1980).

In general, it is difficult to see that any or all of the above mechanisms operates perfectly. Zoning with compensation exists hardly at all, and bribery is surely a hit-and-miss kind of mechanism, Coase (1960) notwithstanding. And a jurisdiction will maximize property value, rather than the median value of property owned by current residents, only if it owns at least some of the financial claims on the development of currently vacant land (as in the case of planned communities (see Henderson, 1980)). But when the vacant land is in absentee private hands, or in a small number of hands, it seems likely that the jurisdiction will be more concerned with the value of its constituents' developed property and largely indifferent to the value of undeveloped land.

In summary, the theory provides us with a statement of the mechanism whereby efficient prices are established, and tells us how to interpret the empirical evidence. Furthermore, we have a statement of a set of forces which tend to result in an efficient price structure. But the ultimate outcome is theoretically indeterminate.

3. Redistribution. The degree of capitalization is of interest independent of its implications for efficient pricing. To a good approximation, fiscally advantaged houses are low-income houses (since within a jurisdiction property taxes rise with property value, which rises with income). Zero capitalization means that the poor do indeed get their local public services more cheaply than do rich people (lower taxes not offset by capitalization). Full capitalization means that everybody gets what he pays for (no redistribution) and more than full capitalization implies perverse redistribution. This result on redistribution of welfare must be modified if there are important within-jurisdiction differences in tastes. But if people segregate themselves by demand for public services this should not be of great importance.

4. Evidence. Though there is some divergence in the empirical work, researchers have typically found close to 100% capitalization. After making adjustments suggested by commentors on his original paper (see Pollakowski, 1973), Oates (1969, 1973) found roughly full capitalization in a cross-section of New Jersey municipalities. (His finding is that a balanced-budget increase in expenditure leaves property values unchanged.) Grether and Mieszkowski (1974) find capitalization of within-jurisdiction variation in quality of schools. (They use direct indices of school rather than expenditure, so we cannot infer the degree of capitalization from their work.) Hamilton (1979) finds roughly 60% capitalization of within-jurisdiction tax variation, using micro data for metropolitan Toronto.

5. Conclusion. To summarize, the theoretical literature is ambiguous as to the degree to which the property tax is transformed into an average cost price. But the empirical literature, finding roughly 100% capitalization, indicates that in practice average cost pricing prevails to a good approximation. Consumers face a set of prices which induce them to make efficient choices given the opportunities available to them, and as a consequence of this there is essentially no income redistribution through the local fisc.

The temptation at this point is to observe that Tiebout was right, and to go home. Indeed, this is the course I have taken (as have others, I hasten to add) in the past. Yet the efficiency question inherent in the title of this paper is deeper. In particular, the literature discussed above almost completely ignores two critical efficiency questions--supply side efficiency and the special costs associated with the Tiebout market-clearing mechanism itself. I devote the next two subsections of my paper to these topics.

B. *Supply*

There are two separate questions regarding supply: (1) Do suppliers offer to demanders the menu of services which is demanded, given the *actual* costs of production, and (2) do suppliers combine inputs efficiently in the process of producing these output bundles? The Tiebout literature addresses the first of these questions, and the empirical literature suggests that demanders are offered an efficient menu. But the Tiebout literature is almost silent on the second question, and the only empirical evidence I am aware of comes from a completely non-Tiebout branch of the literature. The failure of the literature to focus on efficient use of inputs is unfortunate, since this is surely the area of greatest popular discontent with local government.

1. Efficient Offerings. The capitalization literature tells us that public service offerings are roughly what people demand. Otherwise, excess supply or demand for any bundle would be capitalized into property values in a way that would be empirically different from that which is in fact oberved (for discussion of this point see Hamilton, 1976b; Edel and Sclar, 1974; Goldstein and Pauly, 1979). In particular, public service bundles in short supply would command a premium relative to those in excess supply. Thus if there were a chronic tendency to provide more schooling than is demanded, the tax and expenditure coefficients in a capitalization regression would imply that an increase in school expenditure financed by an increase in taxes would lead to a decline in property values. But, as I noted, the bulk of the empirical literature finds that the effect of a balanced budget change is a wash. The obvious implication of this finding is that there is no surplus to be gained by expanding the size of one community type at the expense of another.

Indeed, it would be astonishing if the bundles supplied were other than the bundles demanded, at least roughly. Households can vote not only with their feet but also with their ballots. It is hard to imagine that public officals can tax their citizens either more or less than they want (all things considered) and remain in office. Though there is a great deal that voters may not know about the workings of the public sector, it is hard to imagine that they are ignorant as to whether they are on their own demand curves. I will return to this point in my discussion of Leviathan, below.

It is theoretically plausible, and appears to be true empirically, that the combination of foot and ballot voting does a good job of putting consumers on their demand curves and inducing local governments to offer those bundles which people demand.[6]

2. *Efficient Use of Inputs.* The only theory in the spirit of Tiebout which addresses the input-efficiency question is that of Portney and Sonstelie (1980). They observe that a government which wishes to maximize aggregate property value in its jurisdiction will offer the level of public services which commands the highest rent (if everybody does this we have already seen that ultimately local-fisc-induced differences in rent or property value will be eliminated by competition) and that it will use the most efficient available technology. They note that any failure to efficiently produce and provide services results in a lost opportunity to increase aggregate net rent (or property value). Property value maximization in the Tiebout world plays the same role as profit maximization in the perfect-competition model.

In my view, the Portney-Sonstelie paper completes the basic Tiebout model. We now have an explicit and complete model where (1) consumers are on their demand curves, (2) suppliers offer the bundles which are demanded, and (3) producers use inputs in a technically efficient manner.

III. CHALLENGES TO THE ORTHODOXY

A. *Traditional Challenges*

1. *Scale Economies or Diseconomies.* The mechanism described above is one of average-cost pricing. The efficiency of this price is open to question if average cost diverges from marginal cost; *i.e.*, if there are nonconstant returns to scale. (Note that the returns to scale question refers to the effect upon input requirements of changes in the size of the served population rather than the effect of a change in the quality of delivered service: Can twice the population be served at twice the total cost?) The problems introduced by nonconstant returns are not materially different from those associated with nonconstant returns in a market eco-

[6]Oakland (1979) argues convincingly that California's Proposition 13 was a response to the fact that Californians had been forced off their demand curves as a result of the rapid inflation of the 1970's combined with a very elastic tax structure.

nomy, and need not be discussed here. There are, however, some peculiarities of local government which ought to be noted.

If the average cost curve is steeply U-shaped, it is plausible that an optimal assignment of households to jurisdictions (say, minimum-average-cost population in each of two jurisdictions) will be unstable, and that Tiebout-style behavior will cause the entire population to be dumped into one jurisdiction (see Rose-Ackerman, 1979, esp. pp. 329-330). The same point applies to city size (Henderson, 1980) and to regional migration (Flatters, Henderson, and Mieszkowski, 1974).

Second, there seems to be a mistaken view in the literature that nonconstant returns in the provision of local public goods is qualitatively different from nonconstant returns in ordinary production. Thus for example, Buchanan and Goetz (1972) claim that there are efficiency limits inherent in the Tiebout model as a result of publicness (shared use of a facility) and congestion. But these forces are the standard determinants of the U-shaped *short-run* average cost curve. The shared-use effect they describe is simply the (short-run) fixed input, and congestion is the law of diminishing returns. A recognition that the size of the fixed facility can be altered in the long run removes any *presumption* of the importance of either publicness or crowding in the long run.[7]

Empirically there seems to be no real substance to the (technical) nonconstant returns argument. Bergstrom and Goodman (1973) and Borcherding and Deacon (1972) have both found constant returns for communities of greater than 10,000 population, and I am aware of no counterevidence. Thus neither the possibility of inefficient average-cost pricing nor instability would appear to be of substantial importance.

Much of the richness and complexity of the results presented by Stiglitz (in this volume) is due to the presumption of nonconstant returns. The same point, I believe, applies to Bewley's (1981) critique. His "uninteresting" case of "pure public services" most closely captures reality.

Similarly, Rose-Ackerman (in this volume) makes a great deal of scale economies and congestion. U-shaped cost curves are the main contributors to fiscal externalities associated with migration, and many of the problems of non-existence of equilibrium arise as a result of the same assumption. Interestingly, none of these authors refers to any evidence on the importance of nonconstant returns.

[7]*The same confusion has surrounded discussions of highway pricing. For an excellent statement of the (non) problem, see Mohring (1965).*

But there is a related problem which may be of considerable importance. If scale economies are exhausted at or below 10,000 population then it is possible to have enough jurisdictions to offer a wide variety of choices, even in quite small urban areas. But the mechanism for creating and altering jurisdictions (whatever it is) does not seem to be well suited to doing this. The average population in most of our urban areas offers their residents no more than four or five communities to choose from. Thus many people are forced either above or below their demand curves. Bradford and Oates (1974) have estimated the deadweight loss associated with restricted choice under a variety of assumptions. I am aware of no economic theory of community formation (other than that of Henderson (1980), which covers only special cases), and casual observation suggests that it is a whimsical process. This is unfortunate, because the Bradford-Oates evidence indicates that the process of community formation has significant efficiency implications. Rose-Ackerman argues that the insufficient-offerings problem, even if it doesn't arise from scale economies (and therefore does not create fiscal concern over numbers of residents) can interfere with the formation of a second-best equilibrium (optimal allocation of people among the suboptimal number of communities).

2. *Dynamics*. Much of the paper by Rose-Ackerman (in this volume) is concerned not with the characteristics of an equilibrium but rather the behavior of the system when out of equilibrium. For example, the distribution of capital gains and losses is of concern only when capital gains and losses are being generated--*i.e.*, while prices are changing. And, therefore, the differences between owners and renters is also of importance only while adjustments are taking place. In a steady state, the only difference between owners and renters is that the latter pays his property taxes through the landlord. The renter is willing to pay a premium rent under the same conditions that the homeowner is willing to pay premium house-value plus taxes--the housing plus public services are worth the premium.

Indeed, the way Hamilton and others have been able to avoid the political considerations central to Rose-Ackerman's work is to focus on a steady state which is indeed an equilibrium and an optimum. The real problem with these models is that we have no adequate theory dealing with the behavior of the system away from this optimum. It seems to me that it is the analysis of disequilibrium and adjustment that awaits the integrated economic-political models discussed by Rose-Ackerman.

3. Externalities. Obviously, if the activities of local governments generate externalities, the standard efficiency rules break down and well-known remedies are called for. Public safety and education seem to be the most likely candidates for such externalities. But on close examination, neither seems to be all that important. If benefits of police protection spill out to surrounding communities, then this should be evident in a Bergstrom-Goodman scale effect (annex the surrounding neighborhoods and perceived optimal police expenditure will rise), and the apparent lack of any such effect must reduce the credibility of the externality argument. With regard to education, the relevant question is not whether the benefits are external to the jurisdiction but whether they are external to the direct recipient (the one who votes for, and pays for, the education). The fact that the children move away from the community is irrelevant; it was their parents, not the "community," that bought the education.

In short, I cannot find externalities of any more importance in the local fisc than in the private sector, and I cannot see advocating remedies until there is firm quantitative evidence of a problem.

4. Non-Optimal Equilibria. Several authors have recently pointed out that it is possible to get non-optimal equilibria in a Tiebout world. The example in Rose-Ackerman (in this volume) is identical to that of Bewley (1981), so I can discuss both at once. There are 10 high-demanders and 10 low-demanders of local public services, and no scale economies. Efficiency requires perfect segregation. But suppose by accident that each of the two jursidictions has 5 of each type of demander, and that both jurisdictions agree to provide a level of service halfway between the two demanded levels. Nobody has an incentive to move, because the two jurisdictions are identical.

But on a bit of reflection, this is clearly an unimportant case, as the inefficient "equilibrium" will come unraveled at *any* random shock. If one jurisdiction spends even slightly more than the other, it will attract all the high spenders and repel all the low spenders. So for instance if a new person moves into either of the communities, and demands any expenditure level other than the prevailing compromise, the system will slide into a segregated (efficient) equilibrium. Or to state it differently, from any starting point other than perfect integration, the system will move not toward the integrated, but rather toward the segregated outcome. The Bewley/Rose-Ackerman inefficient equilibrium is in equilibrium in the same sense that a pencil standing on its point is in equilibrium.

B. Leviathan

The major fundamental challenge to the Tiebout literature comes from a group of economists (see Brennan and Buchanan, 1979; Buchanan, 1977) who argue that the coercive power of government imbues it with an element of monopoly power, which is frequently if not generally used to enhance the utility of the elected at the expense of the electorate. The argument is that officials have objectives which differ from those of the electorate, and that they have sufficient monopoly power to pursue these objectives, at least to some degree. There is nothing inherently local about these models, but the proponents do offer their wares in the local public finance literature.

The divergence of officials' objectives from those of the electorate can take one of three forms--(1) efficient provision of public services beyond that level demanded by the public; (2) explicit diversion of tax revenues to private use, via expense account padding, and the like; and (3) (enunciated by Ott, 1980) a setting in which bureaucrats desire to maximize the size of their bureaucracies, and are able to do so by using resources inefficiently (the output of the agency is not excessive, hence it is not a candidate for budget cutting).

1. Inefficient Output Levels. It seems implausible that in a representative government consumers would be willing to be systematically forced above their demand curves, and we have already seen that the empirical evidence contradicts the conjecture. For completeness, however, I note that the proffered mechanism whereby officials pursue this goal is manipulation of the referendum (or equivalent) process. Thus propositions are alleged to be offered to the electorate on an all-or-nothing basis (carefully arranged so that "all" beats "nothing") rather than on the more efficient incremental basis.

Romer and Rosenthal (R&R) (in their paper in this volume and in their previous work cited therein) offer a more complete version of the agenda-setter's monopoly model, and also have provided the most careful empirical support for the Leviathan models. I will remark briefly on their theoretical model, and then turn to the empirical evidence.

R&R expand upon the original Niskanen (1971) version of the agenda setter model by incorporating uncertainty (regarding the outcome of referenda) and the possibility of follow-up referenda in the event the first election fails. This reduces officials' risk of submitting large proposed budgets to the electorate. If it is rejected, a smaller budget can be submitted in a subsequent special election. Officials simply start high and work their way down until they find the highest budget which is preferred to the automatic reversion level (frequently assumed to be some expenditure level substantially below that preferred by the median voter). I have problems with this model because the authors assume voters are unaware that officials can resubmit a budget proposal if the first one is rejected (apparently voters retain this ignorance even after officials have returned to the electorate repeatedly in attempts to get budget proposals passed). Specifically, their statement of consumer behavior is "... we assume that a citizen who votes, votes no if and only if he prefers the (automatic) reversion to the proposal." But if the citizen knows that a rejection of the budget will be followed by another (probably lower proposal), then he ought to vote no so long as he would rather spend less than the proposal. In other words, by imbuing the electorate with a rudimentary understanding of the behavior of public officials (an understanding which is acquired simply by reading the headlines on the front page of the local paper) the R&R model is converted to the median voter model.

Finally, note that the R&R model does not allow for the fact that the officials themselves must stand for reelection. And an election majority can be carved out by the opposition so long as the incumbents' budget exceeds that demanded by the median voter.

Based upon study of Oregon school districts, R&R offer several empirical observations in support of the Leviathan model. First, they find that the expenditure level is statistically associated with the reversion rate. In particular, for those school districts in which the reversion level is so small that the schools would have to close down, expenditure is 15% higher than for those districts in which the reversion level is sufficient to keep the schools open. Closing the schools is of course a rather extreme threat; nationwide it is surely very rare for this to be the outcome of a budget defeat. My own view is that if this extreme threat brings forth only a 15% change in expenditure, the threats which public officials are generally able to embody in reversion levels must have very small effects.

The second piece of evidence cited by R&R is the so-called flypaper effect--unrestricted intergovernmental grants to school districts (and to local governments in general) tend to stick where they land, even though they are legally fungible. Only about 10% of increases in own income go into the local public budget, but of unrestricted grants, almost half (100% by R&R estimate) remain in the local fisc. R&R argue grants remain in the treasury, in opposition to the wishes of the people, because officials fail to inform the electorate about the grant source of income.

I have argued elsewhere (Hamilton, forthcoming-a) that a competing argument is more plausible. One of the inputs in the provision of local public services (schools in particular) is the "quality" of the residents, as argued by Oates (1981). Assume own income is a proxy for this quality. Then own income is a substitute for direct expenditure in the production of education but grants, not being a proxy for quality, are not a substitute for purchased inputs. Thus grants may have a larger effect upon public expenditure than own income. I find this to be a more plausible explanation than the appeal to consumer ignorance, in part because there is substantial independent evidence of the importance of income and other socioeconomic variables in the production of education (see Henderson, Mieszkowski, and Sauvageau, 1978; Oates, 1977).

Finally R&R note that budget proposals frequently pass with large majorities in very small school districts, but are commonly either defeated or pass with small majorities in larger districts. They (correctly, I believe) argue that this pattern exists because officials in large districts start by offering large budgets to the electorate, and work their way down until one passes. Because of the easier flow of information, this does not occur in very small districts. But I do not see Leviathan in these findings. Starting with a big proposal and working down until one passes may simply be the most efficient way of gathering information about consumers' preferences. If all parties know the system works this way, I have already argued that the outcome will be median-voter. And it seems to me this is not a very costly way for officials to learn where the median preference is.

2. Inefficient Input Use. The second possible source of inefficient supply, failure to efficiently convert all inputs into demanded outputs, cannot be refuted by the capitalization literature. Here, all we know empirically is that there are not major differences (within the samples observers have looked at) in the amount of slippage between the taking of inputs and the delivery of outputs (such differences would be capitalized into property values). Ott (1980) offers an empirical test of a model of local government in which individual bureaus have a degree of monopoly power, but the test of monopoly power is very restricted, and in no way does the test rule out the absence of monopoly. Aside from this, I am aware of no empirical literature (aside from the capitalization literature) offered either by the Leviathan proponents or detractors.

Leviathan is a story of officials' ability to thwart the wishes of the voters and escape unscathed (reelected). And it is a set of theories of government which are not inherently local. Indeed, had the timing of contributions to the literature been reversed, we could think of the Tiebout literature as a purely local-government response to Leviathan instead of Samuelson. The peculiarity of local government, emphasized by Tiebout and ignored by Leviathan, is the possibility of foot-voting. And foot-voting is an important check, beyond that offered by ballot-voting, on the monopoly power of government.

3. An Alternative Leviathan Model. In this section I will sketch out a model of local government which will have something of the Leviathan government-failure flavor. I claim its superiority over Leviathan in that (i) it is explicitly local in nature (it considers the discipline imposed by capitalization and foot-voting) and (ii) its assumptions are more compelling (because they are weaker) than those of Leviathan. To call this a model is perhaps over-dramatic--my purpose is to examine the mechanism whereby competitive firms optimize, and to see how well we can expect this mechanism to work in a Tiebout world, even under the best of circumstances.

In long-run competitive equilibrium all firms are using inputs in a technically efficient way and are producing demanded bundles of goods for one very compelling reason: those firms which were not so behaving are bankrupt. More to the point, the forces which drive a competitive system toward this equilibrium are potent. There is an automatic replacement of inefficient firms, and the replacement firm, by the nature of the replacement process, is more efficient. And once long-run equilibrium is approached, the margin for management error becomes very small as maximum profit approaches zero.

How completely does this ruthless automatic-replacement mechanism carry over to the Tiebout mechanism? To answer this question, first note that the immediate consequence of a failure to use inputs efficiently in a Tiebout world is a decline in property value. But note further that the property value decline is sure to be rather modest. If efficiency were to decline 50%, we would expect the jurisdiction's property values to decline about 10%.[8]

The next question is whether we can expect the property value decline to generate the same response that failure to optimize generates in the competitive economy. In short, will the government (*i.e.*, the elected or appointed officials) *automatically* be replaced by a government which is

---

[8]*Assume the property tax goes from 10% to 20% of property value and services are unchanged. Property value would decline by the change in the tax--10%.*

more efficient? The answer is obviously no. At most the government will be replaced in the next election by a government which *promises* to be more efficient and at least it will not be replaced at all. Neither detection of inefficiency nor replacement by greater efficiency is automatic or even particularly likely. The former requires conscious (and considerable) effort on the part of the electorate, and the expected return to gathering this information is modest for any one voter.

Note in particular that foot-voting contributes nothing to this winnowing-out mechanism. A migrant would be as happy to move into an inefficient as an efficient jurisdiction, so long as the difference is fully capitalized. And a current homeowner gains nothing by threatening to move to a more efficient community (if he moves he takes a capital loss; if he stays he takes the same loss as a stream of higher taxes or lower services).

To conclude this mini-model, we have the following result. Even if public entrepreneurs pursue technical efficiency with the same zeal and effectiveness as their private counterparts, the effectiveness of the mistake-correcting device is so much lower in the public sector that we can expect lower average efficiency even if public officials are benevolent dictators, so long as we assume them to be no wiser than private entrepreneurs. Thus we get a Leviathan-like result without ensuring it ahead of time by building avarice and deceit into the model. I do not wish to deny the existence of avarice and deceit, but I do believe the result is strengthened by my lack of reliance on this assumption.[9]

4. Empirical Evidence on Local Government Inefficiency. How important, quantitatively, is local government allocative inefficiency? To my knowledge, there is only one serious piece of research on this topic (Hulten, 1980), and even this work addresses a somewhat less ambitious question. Hulten's task is to estimate the rate of technical change in the state and local sector over the period 1959-1978. Research has been sparse on this question because of the virtual impossibility of measuring output. But Hulten nicely skirts this question by setting up a supply, demand, and market-clearing

---

[9]*Another area in which the private economy is superior to even the best Tiebout economy is innovation. A private entrepreneur can hope to become wealthy from the quasi-rents resulting from an innovation, but a successful innovation merely increases the (already-high) chance of reelection for a public official. In each case, the downside chance is going out of business, so the appropriate comparison is on the payout resulting from success.*

model, and then solving it for a reduced form equation in which the output drops out. Thus he is able to estimate the demand elasticities with respect to price, the coefficients of the technology (competitive shares of capital and labor) and the rate of technical change using only observable variables. (To say the variables are all observable is a bit glib; the task does require construction of time series on the capital and labor stocks utilized by the state and local sector over the sample period.) According to Hulten's estimates, the aggregate state and local sector suffered technical *regress* over the sample period at an annual rate of approximately 1.5%.

Though this does not tell us how well state and local governments are doing as compared with the best available technology, the result states rather forcefully that at least at the end of the sample period we are a long way from the frontier.

This work is new, and to date the only available results treat the entire sector as a unit. But the technique can be applied to individual government units, and Hulten believes that efficiency level comparisons can be made across units. Thus we have hope for empirical determination of which governmental units are most efficient, and what causes differences in efficiency. We might learn which of a variety of factors contributes to (in)efficiency including population size, fiscal distress (it might plausibly work in either direction), governmental structure, income, or any other characteristics of residents.

C. *The Shopping Mechanism*

One of the salient features of the Tiebout mechanism is that the public-service and residential-location consumption decisions are tied to one another. A related feature is that the public service must be consumed in concert with those who share residence in a jurisdiction. Each of these features of the system raises efficiency obstacles which have been largely ignored in the literature.

1. The Location Decision. Residential location decisions involve tradeoffs which are much more subtle than the rent-access tradeoff of monocentric models. Among the complexities are the extra constraints imposed upon two-worker households, and the special problems posed by the passage of time and cost of relocating. Considering the latter, there is evidence (Dynarski, 1981; Dunn, 1979) that neighborhood attachment has substantial value, and that households generally suffer large utility losses when they move. A dramatic illustration of the apparent complexity of the location decision is offered by Hamilton (forthcoming-b). For a sample of 18 SMSA's, I estimated the mean one-way commute which would occur if all workers behaved in accordance with the optimization problem underlying the monocentric model. For cities with available data, the mean actual one-way commute is almost 10 times as large as the "optimal" commute (mean optimum = 0.95 miles vs. actual commute = 7.75 miles). An excellent predictive model for length of commute is one in which people choose their homes and job sites at random, and then commute between the randomly chose sites (my estimate of the mean random commute is 8.6 miles). The observation I wish to make here is that Tiebout shopping (shopping for schools, largely) adds to the complexity of what is already a complicated decision.

Though the necessity of transporting children from home to school automatically ties the residential and school location decisions to some degree, it is obvious that the Tiebout system of local government (as it actually exists) ties the knot more tightly than is technically required.

Another piece of research that emphasizes the complexity of the location decision is McGuire (1974). He observes that private-sector enterprises generally require cooperation among various types of workers, and that in equilibrium these worker types would receive different wages. But the Tiebout paradigm calls for residential segregation by demand for public service (which to a good approximation is segregation by income). Thus there will be efficiency losses, either in private production or in public-service consumption, if everybody who works in a given jurisdiction also lives there. Thus (this goes beyond McGuire's own observations on his model) the Tiebout mechanism, with its attendant segregation, of necessity gives at least some households an incentive not to live near their jobs.

2. A Noneconomic Cost of the Tiebout Mechanism. It has frequently been observed that market or quasi-market provision of primary and secondary education is repugnant for reasons that go far beyond questions of efficiency or income distribution.[10] One of the basic threads in our social fabric is the notion of equal opportunity and equal access to the skills which make us successful citizens. Inherent in this notion is the idea of this country as a place where success depends upon ability and ambition and inter-class mobility is high. One of our ideals is the notion that we do not have a self-perpetuating upper class. And, at least in

[10]*For example, Edwin Mills stressed this point in his comments at the Peterkin Symposium.*

American mythology, the public school system is seen as the great leveler (presumably leveling up, not down). But if a set of ancillary institutions has arisen which has transformed public schools into essentially private schools with average-cost tuition, then the school system is no longer a route through which one can escape his parents' poverty. Perhaps education is one good for which market-like provision ought not be pursued.

3. *Clientele as an Input in Production of Services*. The most fundamental "traditional" challenge to the Tiebout literature is due to Oates (1977, 1981), who argues that the technology for the production of the most important local public services is so unlike that for private goods that we need to rethink both positive and particularly normative aspects of the theory of local public goods. The basic conjecture is that the nature of the constituency itself is an important input in the production of local public services, and furthermore that the substitutability between this input and the traditional purchased inputs is quite low. Oates (1977) cites some evidence in support of his conjecture, and also argues convincingly that it is plausible.

He correctly observes that this phenomenon strengthens the demand on the part of a jurisdiction's residents for exclusionary zoning. At least in a rough sort of way, the descriptive version of the Tiebout model withstands this challenge, though the pricing mechanism is a good deal muddier. The fundamental question concerns efficiency. Here, depending upon the coefficients of the technology, there may be a tradeoff between production efficiency and demand-curve efficiency (Oates gives an example wherein this is true). To be specific but trite, efficiency may require that poor people bribe rich people to go to school with them.

The Oates paper points up vast areas of both theoretical and empirical ignorance, and both sets of questions ought to be high on the profession's research agenda. I think the empirical questions are of somewhat greater importance (if we are able to learn that user-provided inputs are unimportant empirically, then we can ignore the thorny theoretical questions). It seems to me that the Hulten technique provides the most promising vehicle for studying the empirical questions. If we use Hulten's technique to obtain cross-section efficiency-difference estimates, we can then attempt to explain these differences by variations in the characteristics of the population itself--the unmeasured input.

4. *Conclusion*. Aside from the Oates point mentioned above, the following story emerges. The combination of foot and ballot voting does a reasonably smooth job of getting

households on their demand curves for local public services, and of setting supplies equal to demands at average cost prices. The system fails to perform well as a device for ensuring technical efficiency, and the market-clearing mechanism complicates an already complicated residential location decision. These efficiency costs, which have received little attention in the Tiebout literature, may well be very large quantitatively. Hulten's evidence leads me to believe that the efficiency loss is measured not in a few percentage points but in tens of percentage points (possibly several tens).

I believe that the conclusion stated above provides a strong case that further reliance on explicitly private provision of "local public services" would be a Pareto-improving move. It seems that what we have gotten out of our system of local government is a price system without efficency. The system does not provide income redistribution to any significant degree (empirically, average-cost pricing seems to be a good approximation to reality). The system does offer us some efficiency advantages (as compared with central-government provision) through enhanced freedom of choice (see Bradford and Oates (1974) for an estimate of the deadweight loss which would result from uniform provision of education). But arguably the system fails to capture very large efficiency gains which could be had if all of the discipline of the market mechanism were brought to bear. In short, whereas there are strong arguments against providing schools through a market mechanism, these arguments apply with equal force to the (roughly) Tiebout mechanism we seem to have as to a true private market system. But on the other hand, the true market system offers large benefits which our current system foregoes.

REFERENCES

Bergstrom, T. C., and R. P. Goodman, 1973. "Private Demands for Public Goods," *American Economic Review* 63:280-296.
Bewley, T., 1981. "A Critique of Tiebout's Theory of Local Public Expenditures," *Econometrica* 49:713-740.
Bloom, H. S., H. F. Ladd, and J. Yinger, 1982. "Are Property Taxes Capitalized into House Values?", Chapter 7 of this volume.
Borcherding, T. E., and R. T. Deacon, 1972. "The Demand for the Services of Non-Federal Governments," *American Economic Review* 62:891-901.

Bradford, D. F., and W. E. Oates, 1974. "Suburban Exploitation of Central Cities and Government Structure," in H. M. Hochman and G. E. Peterson (eds.), *Redistribution Through Public Choice*. New York: Columbia University Press.

Brennan, G., and J. M. Buchanan, 1979. "The Logic of Tax Limits: Alternative Constitutional Constraints of the Power to Tax," *National Tax Journal* 32 (Supplement):11-22.

Buchanan, J. M., 1977. *Freedom in Constitutional Contract*. College Station: Texas A & M Press.

Buchanan, J. M., and C. J. Goetz, 1972. "Efficiency Limits of Fiscal Mobility," *Journal of Public Economy* 1:25-44.

Coase, R. H., 1960. "The Problem of Social Cost," *Journal of Law Economics* 3:1-44.

deLeeuw, F., 1971. "The Demand for Housing: A Review of Cross-section Evidence," *Review of Economics and Statistics* 53:1-10.

Dunn, C. E., 1979. "Measuring the Value of Community," *Journal of Urban Economics* 6:371-382.

Dynarski, M., 1981. "The Economics of Community," unpublished Ph.D. dissertation, Johns Hopkins University.

Edel, M. D., and E. D. Sclar, 1974. "Taxes, Spending, and Property Values: Supply Adjustments in a Tiebout-Oates Model," *Journal of Political Economy* 82:941-954.

Ellickson, B., 1971. "Jurisdictional Fragmentation and Residential Choice," *American Economic Review 61 (Papers and Proceedings)*:334-339.

Flatters, F., J. V. Henderson, and P. M. Mieszkowski, 1974. "Public Goods, Efficiency, and Regional Fiscal Equilization," *Journal of Public Economics* 3:99-112.

Goldstein, G. S., and M. V. Pauly, 1979. "The Effect of Revenue and Tax Limitation on Property Values," *National Tax Journal* 32 (Supplement):97-104.

Grether, D. M., and P. M. Mieszkowski, 1974. "Determinants of Real Estate Values," *Journal of Urban Economics* 1:127-146.

Hamilton, B. W., 1975. "Zoning and Property Taxation in a System of Local Governments," *Urban Studies* 12:205-211.

Hamilton, B. W., 1976a. "Capitalization of Intrajurisdictional Differences in Local Tax Prices," *American Economic Review* 66:743-753.

Hamilton, B. W., 1976b. "The Effect of Property Taxes and Local Public Spending on Property Values: A Theoretical Comment," *Journal of Political Economy* 84:647-650.

Hamilton, B. W., 1979. "Capitalization and the Regressivity of the Property Tax: Empirical Evidence," *National Tax Journal* 32 (Supplement):169-180.

Hamilton, B. W., forthcoming-a. "The Flypaper Effect and Other Anomalies," *Journal of Public Economics*.
Hamilton, B. W., forthcoming-b. "Wasteful Commuting," *Journal of Political Economy*.
Henderson, J. V., 1980. "Community Development: The Effects of Growth and Uncertainty," *American Economic Review* 70:894-910.
Henderson, J. V., P. M. Mieszkowski, and Y. Sauvageau, 1978. "Peer Group Effects in Educational Production Functions," *Journal of Public Economics* 7:97-106.
Hulten, C. R., 1980. "A Method for Estimating Public Sector Productivity Change," Urban Institute Working Paper.
McGuire, M. C., 1974. "Group Segregation and Optimal Jurisdictions," *Journal of Political Economy* 82:112-132.
Mohring, H., 1965. "Characteristics of an Optimum Transportation System in a Competitive World," in R. Dorfman (ed.), *Measuring the Benefits of Government Investments*. Washington, D.C.: Brookings.
Niskanen, W., 1971. *Bureaucracy and Representative Government*. Chicago: Aldine.
Oakland, W. H., 1979. "Proposition 13--Genesis and Consequences," *National Tax Journal* 32 *(Supplement)*:387-409.
Oates, W. E., 1969. "The Effects of Property Taxes and Local Public Spending on Property Values," *Journal of Political Economy* 77:957-970.
Oates, W. E., 1973. "The Effects of Property Taxes and Local Public Spending on Property Values: A Reply and Yet Further Results," *Journal of Political Economy* 81:1004-1008.
Oates, W. E., 1977. "The Use of Local Zoning Ordinances to Regulate Population Flows and the Quality of Local Services," in W. E. Oates and O. C. Ashenfelter (eds.), *Essays in Labor Market Analysis*. New York: Wiley.
Oates, W. E., 1981. "On Local Finance and the Tiebout Model," *American Economic Review* 71 *(Papers and Proceedings)*:93-98.
Ott, M., 1980. "Bureaucracy, Monopoly, and the Demand for Municipal Services," *Journal of Urban Economics* 8:362-382.
Pollakowski, H. E., 1973. "The Effects of Property Taxes and Local Public Spending on Property Values: A Comment and Further Results," *Journal of Political Economy* 81:994-1003.
Portney, P. R., and J. C. Sonstelie, 1980. "Gross Rents and Market Values: Testing the Implications of Tiebout's Hypothesis," *Journal of Urban Economics* 7:102-118.
Romer, T., and H. Rosenthal, 1982. "Voting and Spending: Some Empirical Relationships in the Policial Economy of Local Public Finance," Chapter 8 of this volume.

Rose-Ackerman, S., 1979. "Market Models of Local Government: Exit, Voting, and the Land Market," *Journal of Urban Economics* 7:319-337.

Rose-Ackerman, S., 1982. "Beyond Tiebout: Modeling the Political Economy of Local Government," Chapter 3 of this volume.

Stiglitz, J. E., 1982. "The Theory of Local Public Goods Twenty-Five Years After Tiebout: A Perspective," Chapter 2 of this volume.

Tiebout, C. M., 1956. "A Pure Theory of Local Public Expenditures," *Journal of Political Economy* 64:416-424.

Chapter 5

THE INCIDENCE OF THE PROPERTY TAX:
THE BENEFIT VIEW VERSUS THE NEW VIEW[1]

George R. Zodrow
Peter Mieszkowski

Department of Economics
Rice University
Houston, Texas

I. INTRODUCTION

Two conflicting views of the incidence of the property tax are prominent in the public finance literature; these views have starkly contrasting implications for the allocative and distributive effects of the tax. The first is the "benefit view" which integrates the local property tax in a Tiebout (1956) framework of perfect consumer mobility and competition among local governments. This approach was pioneered by Hamilton (1975, 1976) who showed how a system of residential property taxes, coupled with either strict zoning ordinances which ensure homogeneous housing or perfect capitalization of property tax differences in house values, is equivalent to a set of non-distortionary user charges. Fischel (1975) and White (1975) extended this approach to property taxes on industrial capital in models where firms are highly mobile between communities and, again with the appropriate zoning ordinances, industrial property tax payments are equivalent to fees for public services.

In contrast, the proponents of a second view, due to the work of Thomson (1965), Mieszkowski (1972), and Aaron (1975), argue that, in general, capital owners bear the burden of the

---

[1]Research support from the National Science Foundation (Grant SES82-09210) is gratefully acknowledged. We have benefited from the comments of Joseph Stiglitz and John Wilson.

property tax, and thus the system of local property taxes is a progressive tax on capital rather than a benefit tax. This "new view" of the property tax takes into account the taxation of both residential and non-residential capital, but is developed independently of any considerations of benefits received from local public expenditures or of zoning. More generally, the new view is based on the general equilibrium incidence model developed by Harberger (1962) for the analysis of national taxes; this approach does not take into account consumer or firm mobility among local jurisdictions offering different expenditure and tax packages. Instead, local property taxes are taken as given and the differential incidence of a national system of local property taxes, relative to a proportional income tax, is determined following what is now fairly conventional methodology (see McLure, 1975).

In this paper, we examine the theoretical approaches which lead to such drastically different results regarding the allocative and distributive effects of the property tax. We focus on two critical differences between the two approaches. First, we consider the importance of zoning (or perfect capitalization) in obtaining the benefit view results. Mobility and interjurisdictional competition, in combination with the appropriate residential and non-residential zoning ordinances, ensure that households and firms are stratified according to demands for public services and located in jurisdictions where tax payments equal public services demanded—or production externalities generated—at the margin. (As stressed by Hamilton (in this volume), perfect capitalization achieves the same result in models where residential zoning does not result in homogeneous housing consumption.) Thus, the distortionary effect of property taxation on capital allocation across jurisdictions, which is one of the critical elements in the derivation of the new view, is eliminated. To illustrate this point, we show that the benefit view result regarding the incidence of the residential property tax can be obtained in a Harberger-type model (which otherwise generates the new view result) simply by imposing the appropriate zoning constraint on housing consumption.

Second, we consider the implications for the new view of the Tiebout-type interjurisdictional competition stressed by proponents of the benefit view. The new view implies that the property tax is a non-benefit tax on capital owners; we inquire whether such exploitation of capital owners can occur once interjurisdictional competition is taken into account. Our approach is to construct a Cournot-Nash model of interjurisdictional competition where each government sets its property tax rate to maximize the welfare of its residents, assuming that all other jurisdictions hold their tax rates fixed. Our model does not allow for production-augmenting effects of local expenditures, as capital is assumed to receive no benefits from local services; capital can be compensated for higher property taxes only by a higher before-tax rate of return. Under these circumstances, as long as each local government has a head tax at its disposal, the optimal tax rate on mobile capital is zero; the competitive equilibrium is not characterized by non-benefit taxation of capital. However, if each government, for statutory, political or other reasons, can finance local public services only through the property tax, the new view result obtains even in a perfectly competitive environment (as the number of local jurisdictions in the economy gets very large). Thus, as long as local governments are constrained to use property tax finance, interjurisdictional competition does not eliminate the exploitation of capital implied by the new view; also, since each government believes the property tax will drive mobile capital out of its jurisdiction, there is a tendency for local governments to provide an inefficiently low level of public services. However, this equilibrium is unstable in the sense that each community can increase the welfare of its residents by reducing its property tax rate and imposing a head tax, as long as all other communities hold their tax rates constant. Thus, to get the new view result within a competitive framework, local governments must be acting myopically or must, for some reason, be prevented from switching from property tax to head tax finance of local services.

We conclude that our analysis suggests that the new view is a viable alternative to the benefit tax explanation of the effects of the property tax; that is, the new view of the property tax has relevance even in a world characterized by interjurisdictional competition, as long as the competition does not extend to the use of head taxes rather than property taxes to finance local public services. Under these circumstances, the property tax has a non-benefit component so that allocative efficiency is impaired and, since this non-benefit component is borne by the owners of capital, the property tax is progressive in comparison to a benefit tax.

II. ZONING, CAPITALIZATION AND THE ALLOCATIVE EFFECTS OF THE PROPERTY TAX

The essential idea underlying the benefit view of the property tax is that perfectly mobile households and firms can move to the community with the public service package that best meets their needs and pay for these services through the local property tax. Since the property tax is effectively a user charge for local public services,[2] the use of the property tax causes no distortions; thus, the resulting equilibrium is allocatively efficient.

A variety of mechanisms can convert the property tax into a user charge. Hamilton (1975) shows that the residential property tax is a benefit tax when consumers are perfectly mobile and residential communities are zoned so that housing is homogeneous; in equilibrium, tastes for public services as well as property tax payments are identical for all households who reside in the community. Hamilton (1976) also shows that perfect capitalization of residential property taxes and services into house values yields the same result in communities with non-homogeneous housing. In both cases, all the households who reside in a community are homogeneous with respect to their demand for local public services.[3] Fischel (1975) and White (1975) demonstrate that the non-residential property tax is a benefit tax when firms are perfectly mobile and communities enact the appropriate non-residential zoning restrictions; public services are treated as another factor of production and the product of the local tax rate and a firm's taxable property equals its public service consumption. In all these cases, households or firms are appropriately stratified so that, at the margin, property tax payments equal local public services received and the resulting equilibrium is allocatively efficient.

Note that the critical element in these analyses is sorting according to demands for public services. Similar results could be obtained for wage or output taxes, as long as the appropriate "zoning" restrictions could be devised and implemented. Thus, in contrast to the new view result that the property tax is a much more progressive tax than a wage tax, the benefit view implies that the substitution of a wage tax for a property tax would, in the long run, have virtually no effect on the distribution of income. Zoning requirements would change and, in some cases, households and firms would have to relocate in order to match property tax payments to benefits received. The benefit view implies that the choice of tax instrument at the local level is largely irrelevant;

[2]*The non-residential property tax can also be viewed as a payment for externalities generated; see Fischel (1975) and White (1975).*

[3]*See the article by Hamilton in this volume for further elaboration.*

with the appropriate zoning ordinances, all tax systems are equivalent to a system of non-distortionary fees for public services.[4]

Thus, one of the key differences between the theoretical analyses yielding the benefit and new views is that in the former case, allocative efficiency is ensured through a variety of zoning or capitalization mechanisms so that the property tax is a non-distorting benefit tax at the margin, while in the latter case, the property tax distorts the capital allocation. This misallocation plays a central role in the Harberger-type differential incidence models which yield the new view result.

To illustrate this point, we consider the incidence of a residential property tax within the context of a Harberger-type model. Our objective is to construct a simple model which demonstrates that without restrictions on the amount of housing consumed, the incidence of a residential property tax is completely on capital and land, as households whose income is solely from wages bear none of the burden of the residential property tax. In contrast, when the amount of housing consumption is restricted by the appropriate zoning ordinances, the residential property tax becomes a lump-sum tax on housing consumption. The burden of the tax is proportional to the amount of housing consumed which, within the context of our model, converts the residential property tax to a benefit tax (as in Hamilton, 1975).

Since we wish to focus on the "average" burden of the tax stressed by Mieszkowski (1972), we consider an economy with a fixed national capital stock and a fixed number of identical local jurisdictions. We assume that each jurisdiction simultaneously uses a residential property tax to finance an increase in publicly provided local services.[5] Each of the representative local jurisdictions in the model is described by the following system of fourteen equations.

Equation 1 shows that a composite good (X) is produced using a Cobb-Douglas production function with capital (K_X), land (V_X) and all the local labor supply (L), while Equation 2 indicates that housing (H) is produced using a Cobb-Douglas production function with capital (K_H) and land (V_H):

$$X = K_X^a V_X^b L^c, \quad a + b + c = 1 \tag{1}$$

$$H = K_H^d V_H^e, \quad d + e = 1. \tag{2}$$

---

[4] See Mieszkowski (1976) for further elaboration.
[5] Thus, we are conducting a "balanced budget incidence" analysis rather than a "differential incidence" analysis; see Musgrave and Musgrave (1980).

Equations 3-5 are the profit-maximizing factor demands; r, s, and w are the net returns to capital, land and labor (capital and land can be used in the production of either the composite good or housing and thus earn the same net return in both uses):

$$K_X = L(a/c)(w/r) \tag{3}$$

$$V_X = L(b/c)(w/s) \tag{4}$$

$$K_H = V_H(d/e)(s/r). \tag{5}$$

Equations 6 and 7 indicate that the fixed stocks of capital (K) and land (V) are fully employed in production of one of the two goods:

$$K = K_X + K_H \tag{6}$$

$$V = V_X + V_H. \tag{7}$$

Equations 8 and 9 are the marginal product pricing equations implied by the assumptions of constant returns to scale production functions and perfectly competitive markets, where q is the price of housing (the composite good is the numeraire with a unitary price $p = 1$) and T is the ad valorem rate of property taxation of the rental values of the capital and land used in the production of residential housing:

$$X = wL + rK_X + sV_X \tag{8}$$

$$qH = (1 + T)(rK_H + sV_H). \tag{9}$$

Government services are treated as "publicly provided private goods."[6] These services are financed in one of two ways. First, the government sells a total of G_1 of the numeraire composite good to its residents, assessing them a user charge of one dollar per unit; in this case, the government is merely a non-profit intermediary which costlessly "transforms" the composite good into public services and sells them to the public. Second, the government provides a total of G_2 of the composite good to its residents, financing the purchase with revenues from the residential property tax; each resident receives G_2/n public services, where n is the population. The case where all public services are financed by user charges ($G_2 = 0$) results in an efficient allocation of resources and serves as a benchmark in the analysis.

[6]For a justification of this treatment of local public goods, see the article by Hamilton in this volume.

The Incidence of the Property Tax

Thus, Equation 10 indicates that all of the composite good is either purchased as a private consumption good (C), sold by the government as public services but financed through user charges (G_1), or provided by the government as public services financed by the residential property tax (G_2). Equation 11 indicates that the government budget for purchases of G_2 must be balanced:

$$X = C + G_1 + G_2 \tag{10}$$

$$G_2 = T(rK_H + sV_H). \tag{11}$$

Finally, Equations 12-14 are the consumer demand equations. All consumers are assumed to maximize a Cobb-Douglas utility function defined over private consumption of the composite good, housing and public services (G_1 and G_2 are perfect substitutes), and all factors are assumed to be locally-owned. Thus, the aggregate consumption demands given in Equations 12-14 can be derived from the maximization of an aggregate Cobb-Douglas utility function

$$U = C^\alpha H^\beta (G_1 + G_2)^\gamma, \quad \alpha + \beta + \gamma = 1,$$

subject to the aggregate income constraint

$$Y = rK + sV + wL = C + G_1 + qH.$$

We assume that all individuals in a jurisdiction have the same income so that each individual receives the same public service level regardless of the choice of tax instrument; thus, any redistribution which occurs in the model results from the tax side, rather than the expenditure side, of the local government budget:

$$C = \alpha(Y + G_2) \tag{12}$$

$$qH = \beta(Y + G_2) \tag{13}$$

$$G_1 + G_2 = \gamma(Y + G_2). \tag{14}$$

Also, in order to focus on the incidence of the property tax in terms of the functional distribution of income, we assume that no individual receives more than one type of factor income; U^K, U^V, and U^L denote the aggregate utilities of capital owners, landowners and labor.

The economy is assumed to be in a zero-tax, undistorted initial equilibrium where all government services are financed by user charges. This assumption implies that the imposition of a residential property tax does not change the level of aggregate utility in the economy.[7]

The incidence of an increase in the residential property tax is analyzed by totally differentiating Equations 1-14 and solving for the changes in the endogenous variables. This procedure yields the factor reallocations caused by the substitution of property tax finance for user charge finance in the model

$$\hat{K}_X = (K_H/K)(1\hat{+}T) \qquad (15)$$

$$\hat{K}_H = -(K_X/K)(1\hat{+}T) \qquad (16)$$

$$\hat{V}_X = (V_H/V)(1\hat{+}T) \qquad (17)$$

$$\hat{V}_H = -(V_X/V)(1\hat{+}T), \qquad (18)$$

where the circumflex indicates logarithmic differentiation; thus, the housing sector shrinks and the composite good sector expands as a result of the residential property tax.

It is straightforward to show that property owners bear the burden of the property tax in this variant of the Harberger model. The utility change experienced by each income group, net of the increase in publicly-provided services which is shared equally by all residents, is

$$dU^i/\lambda - dG_2/n = dY^i - H^i dq, \quad i = K, V, L, \qquad (19)$$

where λ is the common marginal utility of income and Y^i and H^i are the incomes and housing consumption of each income group. Revenues from the residential property tax can be separated into a capital component $R_K = TrK_H$ and a land component $R_V = TsV_H$. Solving for the net utility change for each group of factor owners yields the incidence results

$$(dU^K/\lambda - dG_2/n)/Y^K = -(K_H/K)(1\hat{+}T) = -dR_K/Y^K \qquad (20)$$

$$(dU^V/\lambda - dG_2/n)/Y^V = -(V_H/V)(1\hat{+}T) = -dR_V/Y^V \qquad (21)$$

$$(dU^L/\lambda - dG_2/n)/Y^L = 0. \qquad (22)$$

Thus, capital owners bear the capital component of the residential property tax burden, land owners bear the land compo-

---

[7]At a zero-tax initial equilibrium, excess burden effects are of the second order and thus do not appear in differential incidence expressions; see Ballentine and Eris (1975) and Vandendorpe and Friedlaender (1976).

nent, and labor bears none of the tax. That is, labor benefits from its share of the publicly provided services, but the real income of wage-earners is unchanged by the imposition of the residential property tax (independently of how much of the tax-financed G_2 is distributed to this income group). This new view type result--all capital and land-owners bear the burden of a residential property tax--obtains because labor receives the publicly provided services G_2 by residing in the jurisdiction but reduces its housing consumption in response to the residential property tax. The effect of the resulting factor reallocation is a reduction in the returns to property owners sufficiently large that they bear the entire burden of the tax.

This result is straightforward in the case of Cobb-Douglas utility and production functions. With more general functional forms, the strong result that labor bears none of the burden of the residential property tax does not obtain. Nevertheless, the general tendency for capital and land to bear a disproportionate share of the burden remains. The residential property tax leads to a shrinkage of the housing sector and the shift of capital and land into the composite good sector increases the relative return to labor.

This new view type result hinges on the assumption that there are no zoning constraints on housing consumption. Suppose instead that the local governments require residents to purchase the quantity of housing which maximizes their utility. Since the initial zero-tax equilibrium is Pareto efficient, this is equivalent to imposing the requirement that $\hat{H} = 0$ as the property tax is increased. In this case, an increase in the residential property tax rate has no effect on factor allocation or on factor prices, while housing prices increase by the full amount of the tax,

$$\hat{q} = (1\hat{+}T); \tag{23}$$

households bear the full burden of the property tax financed increase in publicly provided services in proportion to their consumption of housing, which is proportional to income.

Thus, with the appropriate zoning constraint, the model yields the benefit view--consumers of local public services bear the full burden of the residential property tax which finances them. With no excess burden effects, the changes in the levels of utility resulting from the imposition of the residential property tax are all zero.

Finally, note that in the model above, in keeping with the benefit view literature (e.g., Hamilton, 1975), housing consumption is constrained by the zoning ordinances. It is straightforward to show that the benefit view result does not obtain if instead the amount of land used for housing is fixed (e.g., minimum lot zoning) at the value of V_H in the zero-tax equilibrium. Solving the same system of equations subject to the constraint that $\hat{V}_H = 0$ yields the results that capital owners bear the capital component of the residential property tax, while residential land owners bear the land component; the latter result obtains because the zoning constraint prevents a reallocation of land to production of the composite good. Thus, labor and non-residential landowners receive the benefits of publicly provided local services without bearing any burden of the residential property tax when residential land, rather than housing consumption, is subject to a zoning constraint.

III. INTERJURISDICTIONAL COMPETITION AND THE NEW VIEW OF THE PROPERTY TAX

The results in the previous section provide a set of conditions under which a new view result obtains--capital owners bear the full burden of the capital component of a residential property tax. Under these conditions, capital owners are "exploited" in the sense that they pay more in property taxes than they consume in services. The benefit view result regarding the incidence of the residential property tax is obtained within the Harberger framework only when the demand for housing is constrained so that the factor reallocations which lead to the new view type result are ruled out. However, if we modified our model to consider the simultaneous taxation of non-residential and residential capital stressed by Mieszkowski (1972) in the derivation of the new view, constraining housing consumption would not be sufficient to yield the benefit view result; since capital is taxed at the same rate in both production sectors, the exploitation result does not obtain due to a reallocation of capital between sectors. Instead, exploitation occurs because the application of the Harberger fixed national capital stock model to the analysis of a system of local property taxes implies that all local governments simultaneously use the property tax so that capital can not escape the tax--not surprisingly, these assumptions lead to the new view result.

However, the application of the Harberger model to the analysis of a national system of local property taxes is somewhat tenuous because it does not properly take into account either the independence of local governments in setting their own property tax rates or the constraints local governments operate under due to the interjurisdictional competition stressed by proponents of the benefit view. By emphasizing the effects of the average rate of property taxa-

The Incidence of the Property Tax

tion in the nation, the approach poses the question in the context of a simultaneous increase or decrease of the tax by all governments. This "experiment" is suggestive of collusive behavior among local governments, although the mechanism by which this collusion occurs is not specified.

In this section, we present a model that should put the new view on somewhat firmer footing. First, we demonstrate that interjurisdictional competition is inconsistent with non-benefit taxation of mobile capital as argued by proponents of the benefit view, as long as local governments can raise revenues through lump sum taxes. However, if local governments are constrained, for statutory, political or any other reasons, to finance local public services only through property taxes on capital, the new view result obtains. That is, even with perfect competition among jurisdictions, capital owners bear the full burden of the property tax. Moreover, we show that property tax finance leads to an inefficiently low level of local public service provision.

Again, our model is a simple one. To focus on the question of possible non-benefit taxation of capital, we assume that non-residential production uses no local services and generates no externalities. According to the benefit view, non-residential capital should not be taxed. Our approach, following Epple and Zelenitz (1981), is an application of standard industrial organization theory to a model of a national economy with a fixed number (N) of identical local jurisdictions. That is, we determine the level of property taxation chosen by each local government under the assumption that all other local governments hold their property tax rates fixed; perfect competition among local jurisdictions in this Cournot-Nash setting is modeled as the case where the number of jurisdictions becomes very large.

Consider a perfectly competitive economy with a fixed national capital stock where each of the N jurisdictions has a fixed land supply $V = 1$. Equations 24-27 describe a representative jurisdiction i ($i = 1,...N$). Output X_i is produced in each jurisdiction with capital (K_i) and land using a strictly concave, constant returns production function

$$X_i = F(K_i), \quad F' > 0, \quad F'' < 0, \tag{24}$$

where the fixed land argument is suppressed. Marginal product pricing ensures

$$r(1 + T_i) = F'(K_i) \tag{25}$$

where r is the net return to capital which is assumed to be perfectly mobile among the N jurisdictions, T_i is the *ad valorem* property tax rate on capital rental values in jurisdiction i, and output is the numeraire. It will be convenient to define $\tau_i = T_i/(1 + T_i)$ as the tax rate expressed as a percentage of the gross rental payment to capital. The return to landowners is the residual after capital payments

$$S_i = X_i - r(1 + T_i)K_i, \qquad (26)$$

where S_i is the net return to landowners in jurisdiction i and land is not subject to the property tax. Local government services (G_i) are again treated as publicly provided private goods and are modeled as public purchases of output which are financed either with the property tax on capital or with a head tax with total revenue H_i:

$$G_i = T_i r K_i + H_i. \qquad (27)$$

Local services, as well as the head tax, are shared equally by local landowners; the ownership of all land in the jurisdiction is equally divided among these local landowners, who have no other source of income. Note that in this model the head tax is equivalent to a land value tax. The model is closed by imposing the fixed national capital stock constraint:

$$K = \sum_{i=1}^{N} K_i. \qquad (28)$$

Since the local government in each jurisdiction acts on the assumption that all other jurisdictions will not respond to changes in its property tax rate, the effect on the net return to capital expected by a representative jurisdiction j when it increases its property tax rate is obtained by differentiating Equation 25 and substituting into the result of differentiating Equation 28 for $dT_i = 0$, $i \neq j$:

$$\hat{r} = -\varepsilon_{rj}(1 + \hat{T}_j), \qquad (29)$$

where

$$\varepsilon_{rj} = \frac{(1 + T_j)/F''(K_j)}{\sum_i (1 + T_i)/F''(K_i)} > 0.$$

In the Nash equilibrium, when all N jurisdictions behave identically, $\varepsilon_{rj} = 1/N$; as N gets large, ε_{rj} approaches zero, indicating that any individual jurisdiction cannot affect the national rate of return to capital.

The Incidence of the Property Tax

The capital supply elasticity with respect to increases in T_j is obtained by substituting from Equation 29 into the result of differentiating Equation 25:

$$\hat{K}_j = -\varepsilon_{Kj}\,(1\hat{+}T_j), \qquad (30)$$

where

$$\varepsilon_{Kj} = -\frac{r(1+T_j)}{F''(K_j)}\,\frac{(1-\varepsilon_{rj})}{K_j} > 0.$$

The effect of an increase in property taxes on land prices in the jurisdiction is obtained by substituting from Equations 25 and 30 and from the result of differentiating Equation 24 into the result of differentiating Equation 26:

$$\hat{s}_j = -(\theta_{Kj}/\theta_{Vj})\,(1-\varepsilon_{rj})\,(1\hat{+}T_j), \qquad (31)$$

where θ_{Kj} and θ_{Vj} are the capital and land shares in production costs in jurisdiction j. Substituting from Equations 29 and 30 into the result of differentiating Equation 27 yields the differential equation for the government budget constraint:

$$\hat{G}_j = \phi_{Tj}[1/\tau_j - (\varepsilon_{Kj} + \varepsilon_{rj})]\,(1\hat{+}T_j) + \phi_{Hj}\hat{H}_j, \qquad (32)$$

where ϕ_{Tj} and ϕ_{Hj} are the shares of government services financed by property taxes and by head taxes. The revenue-maximizing tax rate for each jurisdiction is thus the inverse of the sum of its capital supply and interest rate elasticities.

The equilibrium for the economy can be calculated once the objective function for each local government is specified. Since we are concerned with the hypothesis of exploitation of capital owners, we adopt the assumption most conducive to such exploitation--local governments act to maximize the welfare of resident landowners. Local residents are assumed to have an identical utility function which is homogeneous of degree one in net income and government services, so the government maximizes the welfare of local resident landowners by choosing H_j and T_j to maximize the same utility function defined over aggregate resident landowner income (Y_j) and government services:

$$U_j[Y_j(H_j,T_j),\,G_j(H_j,T_j)],$$

where

$$Y_j = s_j - H_j;$$

differentiating and substituting from Equation 31 yields:

$$\hat{Y}_j = -\frac{s_j}{Y_j}\frac{\theta_{Kj}}{\theta_{Vj}}(1-\varepsilon_{rj})(1+\hat{T}_j) - \frac{H_j}{Y_j}\hat{H}_j. \qquad (33)$$

The first order conditions for the local government optimization problem[8] indicate that, at the optimum, the marginal rate of substitution between public and private goods (m_j) should be one

$$m_j = (\partial U_j/\partial Y_j)/(\partial U_j/\partial G_j) = 1, \qquad (34)$$

and that the optimal tax rate is implicitly defined by

$$\tau_j = \varepsilon_{rj}/(\varepsilon_{Kj} + \varepsilon_{rj}). \qquad (35)$$

The optimal tax rate thus depends on the extent of interjurisdictional competition in the economy as we have obtained a typical Cournot-Nash result—the extent of appropriation of capital rents varies from none ($\tau_j = 0$) to total ($\tau_j = 1$) as the nature of interjurisdictional competition varies from perfect competition ($\varepsilon_{rj} = 0$) to pure monopoly ($\varepsilon_{rj} = 1$, $\varepsilon_{Kj} = 0$).

Although the oligopoly model ($\varepsilon_{rj} > 0$) may have some relevance if local jurisdictions view the metropolitan capital stock as fixed and the number of competing suburban jurisdictions is relatively small, our principal result is that in a competitive environment the optimal tax on mobile capital is zero; only head taxes (or land value taxes in our model) will be used to finance local expenditures. The explanation for this result is quite straightforward. As the number of communities becomes large, a single community acting in isolation must take the after-tax rate of return as given; any tax on capital increases the supply price of capital by the amount of tax. However, a tax on capital also distorts the allocation of capital and results in an excess burden—by restricting the use of capital, a capital tax lowers output and decreases land rents. Landlords, or more generally the owners of fixed factors, recognize they will bear the burden of a head tax. However, since they are

---

[8] *Our optimal tax formulas are special cases of the results presented by Arnott and Grieson (1981) in their comprehensive treatment of this local government optimal taxation problem.*

unable to exploit capital through non-benefit taxation in any case, the head (benefit) tax is preferred to a distortionary tax on the mobile factor.

Our model thus suggests that the interjurisdictional competition stressed by proponents of the benefit view (as well as by Tiebout) does imply that the property tax will be used only as a benefit tax. However, the model can easily be altered to yield the new view result. Suppose that for statutory, political or other reasons, local governments can raise revenues to finance local public services only through a property tax on capital; there are no head taxes. In this case, even with perfect competition among local jurisdictions, each local government will engage in non-benefit of taxation and the new view result obtains.

Our model is unchanged except that head taxes are constrained to be zero so that the only control variable available to each local government is its property tax rate. In this case, the first order condition for each local government yields the following implicit expression for the optimal tax rate:

$$\tau_j = (1 - m_j)/\varepsilon_{Kj}. \tag{36}$$

The interpretation of this condition is straightforward. At the optimum, the marginal rate of substitution must equal the slope of the perceived "production possibilities frontier" for the representative jurisdiction. The latter, which is obtained by combining Equations 32 and 33 when $H_j = \varepsilon_{rj} = 0$ to yield

$$-dG_j/dY_j = 1 - \tau_j \varepsilon_{Kj},$$

is equal to one at the zero-tax (and zero-service) equilibrium. As long as $m_j < 1$ at the zero tax equilibrium and the production possibilities frontier is concave for tax rates below the revenue-maximizing level, the optimal property tax rate must be positive; we assume these plausible conditions hold for the balance of the discussion.

Thus, when local public services can be financed only through the property tax, the optimal tax is positive, increasing as m_j falls (preferences for public services are strong) and as ε_{Kj} falls (the capital out-migration expected by each local jurisdiction in response to property taxation falls). Since all jurisdictions act identically and the national capital stock is fixed, we obtain the new view result that capital bears the entire burden of the property tax. Moreover, there is a tendency toward underconsumption of public services--$m_j = 1$ at any income level with head tax finance while $m_j < 1$ with property tax finance as local governments reduce services to mitigate the effects of the expected reduction in capital supply, output, and land rents induced by property taxation. However, the net effect on the level of government services (relative to the head tax case) is theoretically ambiguous since in the competitive Nash equilibrium landowners effectively have another source of income with which to purchase public services--expropriated capital rents.

Thus, interjurisdictional competition cannot eliminate the exploitation of capital implied by the new view if the property tax is the sole source of local revenue. However, note that the Nash equilibrium described above can be unstable in the sense that any single jurisdiction has an incentive to impose a head tax and reduce its reliance on the property tax. Suppose that a single jurisdiction, again assuming that all other jurisdictions hold their tax rates fixed, introduces a head tax and reduces its property tax, holding service levels constant. Local resident landowners will benefit from this substitution if

$$dY_j = ds_j - dH_j > 0.$$

Substituting from Equations 31 and 32 when $dG_j = 0$ and evaluating at $H_j = 0$, $\tau_j = (1-m_j)/\varepsilon_{Kj}$ shows that this condition is satisfied:

$$dY_j = rK_j (1 + T_j)(1 - m_j)[-(1+\hat{T}_j)] > 0.$$

The substitution of a non-distorting head tax for a distorting capital tax is desirable for the same reason that property taxes were not used when the head tax was available. Each community, taking the tax rate of all the other communities as given, attempts to obtain an advantage relative to other communities by attracting more capital. The loss in tax revenues resulting from the decrease in taxes on mobile capital is offset dollar for dollar by a decrease in the cost of capital, which in turn induces increases in the local capital stock, output, and land rents.

In general, Equations 35 and 36 are non-linear expressions and cannot be solved explicitly for the optimal property tax rates under the head tax and property tax regimes. However, explicit solutions are straightforward for the case of Cobb-Douglas functional forms, and for illustrative purposes are presented below for the perfectly competitive case ($\varepsilon_{rj} = 0$).

Suppose that the utility and production functions in the model are given by:

$$U_i = Y_i^{\alpha} G_i^{\beta}, \quad \alpha + \beta = 1.$$

$$X_i = K_i^a V^b = K_i^a, \quad a + b = 1.$$

In this case, we can solve for

$$r = aK^{-b} [\Sigma (1 + T_i)^{-1/b}]^b$$

$$K_i = [r(1 + T_i)/a]^{-1/b}$$

$$\varepsilon_{Kj} = \theta_{Vj}^{-1} = 1/b.$$

The optimal tax rate is zero under the head tax regime and is given by

$$\tau_j = b[1 - \alpha b/(\beta + \alpha a)]$$

when the head tax is not available. Equilibrium values for the endogenous variables (when $K = N$) are given in Table I, where the parameter ψ is defined as

$$\psi = a/(a + \beta b) = 1/(1 + T_j), \quad 0 < \psi < 1.$$

Note that when only the property tax on capital can be utilized to raise local revenues, we obtain the new view result—capital bears the entire burden of the property tax

TABLE I. Endogenous Variable Values for a Representative Jurisdiction for the Two Models of Interjurisdictional Competition

Endogenous Variable	Property Tax and Head Tax Available	Only Property Tax Available
τ_j	0	$\beta b/(\beta + \alpha a)$
H_j	βb	0
G_j	βb	$\psi \beta b$
Y_j	αb	b
S_j	b	b
$r(1+T_j)$	a	a
r	a	ψa

as the after-tax rate of return falls by the average rate of tax relative to the head tax case. Note also that the level of government spending is lower with the property tax than it is under the head tax. Thus, in the Cobb-Douglas case, the distortionary effect of the property tax at any income level --local governments cut back on services to avoid expected reductions in the capital stock, output, and land rents-- dominates the income effect associated with the expropriation of capital rents. Finally, note that it is quite possible that the utility of landowners will be higher under the property tax system than under the head tax system even though the level of services is reduced. To see this, note that resident landowner net income is higher in the property tax case than in the head tax case; land rents are the same under the two tax regimes, but under the tax system part of these rents are used to finance public services, whereas in the property tax system all land rents are spent on private goods and expropriated capital rents finance public services. Substituting from Table I yields the result that

$$U_P/U_H \gtreqless 1 \text{ as } \alpha^{-\alpha} \psi^\beta \gtreqless 1,$$

where U_P and U_H are the utility levels of landowners in the representative jurisdiction under the property tax and head tax systems. Although not always the case, landowners' utility is higher under the property tax regime for most plausible parameter values. For example, if ten percent of income is devoted to local public services in the undistorted head-tax equilibrium ($\beta = 0.1$), $U_P/U_H > 1$ as long as the capital share in gross production costs is greater than six percent ($a > 0.06$).

IV. GENERAL EVALUATION AND CONCLUSIONS

Property taxation of capital has not disappeared--the property tax has not been replaced by a system of neutral land value or local head taxes as suggested by the model of competition we have developed.[9] What are we to make of the persistence of property taxes? One explanation is the benefit view of the property tax. The model above makes no provision for benefits associated with capital taxes. Capital is taxed for the benefit of the immobile factors of production (land and possibly labor) and receives no benefits in return. The benefit view suggests that the model we have

[9]*Local use of head taxes has been advocated for reasons other than those presented here; see Mills (1979).*

The Incidence of the Property Tax

developed is incorrect in that interjurisdictional competition, when accompanied by the appropriate zoning restrictions, transforms a set of apparently distorting capital levies into neutral user charges or benefit levies.

Although the internal logic of this argument is unassailable, its grounding in fact is open to question. In particular, the complex pattern of strict zoning ordinances which is required to convert the industrial property tax into a payment for public services received seems to be a rather severe requirement.

An alternative explanation of the persistence of property taxes is that local governments choose not to substitute head taxes or land value taxes for property taxes, even though our results at the end of Section III suggest that it would appear to be in their interests to do so. This may occur for at least three reasons. First, due to legal or political constraints, local governments may simply not be able to make the substitution. Second, local governments may engage in a plausible type of collusion to expropriate rents from capital owners. Our Nash equilibrium with the property tax occurs in a model where jurisdictions compete with respect to tax rates, but the competition does not extend to eliminating the property tax as the source of local revenue; our results suggest that this type of collusion is likely to be profitable in the sense that it benefits all landowners, and the traditional use of the property tax as "the" local tax instrument provides a ready vehicle for this type of collusion. Third, local governments may be fully aware of the implications of perfect capital mobility in the long run, but they may have a shorter time perspective in choosing their tax instruments; since capital is highly durable in the short run, current revenue losses from lower capital taxes may outweigh the long run benefits of higher land rents from the perspective of local government officials. The general point is again that the assumptions which imply the elimination of non-benefit taxation of mobile capital are severe and somewhat unrealistic.

Are local property taxes benefit taxes? They may be--but we remain skeptical. Instead, it seems plausible that there is a non-benefit component to the property taxation of capital which is borne primarily by the owners of capital as predicted by the new view of the property tax.

REFERENCES

Aaron, H. J., 1975. *Who Pays the Property Tax?* Washington, D. C.: Brookings Institution.
Arnott, R., and R. E. Grieson, 1981. "Optimal Fiscal Policy for a State or Local Government," *Journal of Urban Economics* 9:23-48.
Ballentine, J. G., and I. Eris, 1975. "On the General Equilibrium Analysis of Tax Incidence," *Journal of Political Economy* 83:633-644.
Epple, D., and A. Zelenitz, 1981. "The Implications of Competition Among Jurisdictions: Does Tiebout Need Politics?", *Journal of Political Economy* 89:1197-1217.
Fischel, W. A., 1975. "Fiscal and Environmental Considerations in the Location of Firms in Suburban Communities," in E. S. Mills and W. E. Oates (eds.), *Fiscal Zoning and Land Use Controls*. Lexington, Mass.: Lexington Books.
Hamilton, B. W., 1975. "Zoning and Property Taxation in a System of Local Governments," *Urban Studies* 12:205-211.
Hamilton, B. W., 1976. "Capitalization of Intrajurisdictional Differences in Local Tax Prices," *American Economic Review* 66:743-753.
Harberger, A. C., 1962. "The Incidence of the Corporate Income Tax," *Journal of Political Economy* 70:215-240.
McLure, C. E., Jr., 1975. "General Equilibrium Incidence Analysis: The Harberger Model After Ten Years," *Journal of Public Economics* 4:125-161.
Mieszkowski, P. M., 1972. "The Property Tax: An Excise Tax or a Profits Tax?" *Journal of Public Economics* 1:73-96.
Mieszkowski, P. M., 1976. "The Distributive Effects of Local Taxes: Some Extensions," in R. E. Grieson (ed.), *Public and Urban Economics: Essays in Honor of William S. Vickery*. Lexington, Mass.: Lexington Books.
Mills, E. S., 1979. "Economic Analysis of Urban Land-Use Controls," in P. Mieszkowski and M. Straszheim (eds.), *Current Issues in Urban Economics*. Baltimore: Johns Hopkins University Press.
Musgrave, R. A., and P. B. Musgrave, 1980. *Public Finance in Theory and Practice*. New York: McGraw-Hill.
Thomson, P., 1965. "The Property Tax and the Rate of Interest," in G. C. S. Benson, S. Benson, H. McClelland, and P. Thomson, *The American Property Tax*. Claremont, Cal.: The Lincoln School of Public Finance.
Tiebout, C. M., 1956. "A Pure Theory of Local Expenditures," *Journal of Political Economy* 64:416-424.

Vandendorpe, A. L., and A. F. Friedlaender, 1976. "Differential Incidence in the Presence of Initial Distorting Taxes," *Journal of Public Economics* 6:205-229.

White, M. J., 1975. "Firm Location in a Zoned Metropolitan Area," in E. S. Mills and W. E. Oates (eds.), *Fiscal Zoning and Land Use Controls*. Lexington, Mass.: Lexington Books.

Chapter 6

INCOME REDISTRIBUTION IN A FEDERAL SYSTEM

William H. Oakland

Department of Economics
Tulane University
New Orleans, Louisiana

I. INTRODUCTION

Income redistribution at the sub-national level has been given scant explicit attention in the public finance literature.[1] While the Tiebout (1956) mechanism is partly driven by redistributive considerations, income redistribution comes into play only as a by-product of a locality's provision of public services. In the absence of benefit taxation, the finance of local public services will generally involve a transfer from rich to poor. If people are mobile, such a consideration may render the spatial allocation of resources inefficient and may also distort the choice of public services themselves. As Hamilton (1975) has shown, such inefficiencies can be avoided only if communities restrict mobility by zoning or other non-price rationing schemes. In such an event, income redistribution vanishes entirely as people are segregated into homogeneous groups.

Not only do this model's predictions clash violently with reality with respect to income redistribution in the provision of local public services, but its focus upon public service provision masks an important feature of the fiscal landscape. That is, sub-national units, particularly state governments, engage in *direct* income redistribution through such programs as public assistance, food stamps, publicly

[1] *For an exception, see Pauly (1973).*

subsidized housing, and health insurance.[2] The literature has been relatively silent on these activities, even though they absorb a significant fraction of state-local own-tax revenues. The orthodoxy, if there is one, is stated in Oates' (1972) treatise on Fiscal Federalism.[3] In effect, he hypothesizes that redistribution can be carried out at the sub-national level only at the risk of the economic viability of the redistributing government. For a government which pursues redistribution in an aggressive manner will tend to lose its affluent population to other regions and, at the same time, attract the poor from other areas. For these reasons, the orthodoxy states that sub-national units will not do "enough" redistribution for equity purposes, and to the extent that they do redistribute, the spatial allocation of resources will be distorted. Thus, the conclusion of orthodox public finance is that redistribution is best left to the central government.

But this prescription is deficient on both normative and positive grounds. Because of regional differences in living costs and other amenities it is likely that a system of uniform welfare transfers will fall short of the mark needed for equity in high cost areas and above it in low cost areas. Moreover, the orthodoxy fails to predict the pattern of division of responsibility which has emerged--*i.e.*, sub-national units do play an important role in the finance of current welfare programs. In part, this failure is due to the exaggerated role assigned to mobility in response to regional cost differentials. While appropriate, perhaps, for the intra-urban allocation of population, there is much less justification for it in the interregional allocation. Evidence suggests that regional living standard differences can persist for very long periods of time. Hence, state governments do not have to operate under the assumption that an above average welfare program will lead immediately to its impoverishment. Rather, as the vastly different social welfare levels of New York and Mississippi indicate, states can pursue independent policies toward income redistribution.

The objective of this paper is to explore how the policies of national and sub-national redistributive programs interact so as to determine an overall distribution of income. Not only is this an interesting question in its own right, but it has relevance to the current proposal to return responsibility for welfare to the states. Our approach will be to develop several simple models in order to identify those institutions and circumstances under which states will find it desirable to supplement federal welfare programs.

[2] For a discussion of this process, see Oakland (1979).
[3] See Oates (1972), Chap. 1.

The analysis will be based upon the assumption of citizen immobility. While less than ideal, this assumption vastly simplifies the analysis and offers a substantive alternative to those results which depend on perfect mobility.

II. THE MODEL

We assume a world with two classes of individuals--the rich (R) and the poor (P). There is a continuum of communities of equal size which differ only in the proportion of their population which is poor (n).

Communities are distributed according to the function

$$F(n) = \int_0^n f(n)dn, \quad 0 \leq n \leq 1.$$

To begin, we assume the pre-tax income of both the rich and poor to be fixed at R and P, respectively. Each individual has an identical, strictly concave utility function $[U(\cdot)]$ which depends only upon that individual's disposable income, R^D or P^D. Governments, local as well as national, can impose a proportional income tax and spend the proceeds to offer a demogrant (G) to each of its citizens. Hence, disposable income is

$$Y^D(n) = Y[1 - t_L(n) - t_F] + G_L(n) + G_F, \quad Y = R, P, \qquad (1)$$

where t is the proportional tax rate, G is the demogrant, and the subscripts refer to the local and federal levels of government.[4]

Each local government is assumed to maximize the additive welfare function

$$W_L(n) = nU(P^D) + a(1 - n)U(R^D), \quad a > 1. \qquad (2)$$

Notice that the utility of the rich carries a weight greater than unity. This is assumed for two reasons. First, if $a = 1$, each local government would set $t_L = 1$ and there would be no role left for the federal government. The problem is thus trivial. Second, $a > 1$ reflects the fact that the mobility and/or tax avoiding opportunities of the rich are

---

[4]*Equivalently, we could imagine that governments impose a tax (T = tR - G) on the rich and give a subsidy (S = G - tP) to the poor. In other words, the policy parameters t and G are sufficient to realize any desired level of redistribution.*

greater than for the poor. While we will formalize tax avoidance later, $a > 1$ offers a useful approximation. Hence, local governments will not go so far as total equality.

The problem confronting the local government is to maximize (2) subject to

$$t_L(n)\,\mu(n) = G_L(n), \tag{3}$$

where $\mu(n) = nP + (1 - n)R$ is average community income. We assume that the tax rate cannot be negative, so we have the inequality constraint

$$t_L(n) \geq 0. \tag{4}$$

Assuming (4) to be non-binding, we obtain at the maximum

$$aU'(R^D) = U'(P^D), \tag{5}$$

where $U'(R^D)$ and $U'(P^D)$ are the marginal utilities of income for the rich and poor, respectively. Clearly, $a > 1$ implies $R^D > P^D$.

The solution of the local government problem is shown in Figure 1. The community's budget constraint is

$$P^D = \mu(n)/n - [(1 - n)/n]R^D. \tag{6}$$

From (2), the slope of the community indifference curve is

$$dP^D/dR^D = -a[(1 - n)/n]\,[U'(R^D)/U'(P^D)]. \tag{7}$$

Inspection of (6) indicates that the slope of the community's budget constraint is a decreasing (in absolute value) function of the proportion of poor. In Figure 2 we show the budget lines for three types of communities: a rich community with $n < \int sf(s)ds = \bar{n}$; the average community with $n = \bar{n}$; and a poor community with $n > \bar{n}$. These curves are given by rr', aa', and pp', respectively. If P^D and R^D are normal goods, i.e., a lump-sum transfer to the community causes it to adopt greater P^D and R^D, the locus of community equilibria will fall along a rising curve such as EE' in Figure 2. That is, the disposable income of both the rich and poor will be greater the lower a community's n. Thus, the more affluent communities will provide greater redistributive benefits to their poor, but the increased redistribution will never be so great as to make the rich worse off than in a community with higher n.

The equilibrium locus EE' is upward sloping since it is on the income expansion path for every community. This is due to the fact that the tangency condition (5) is indepen-

Income Redistribution in a Federal System

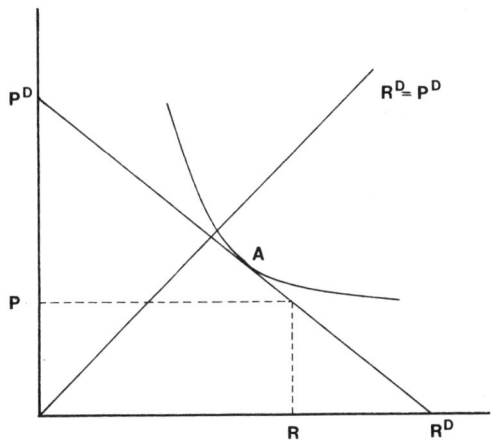

FIGURE 1. *The local government equilibrium.*

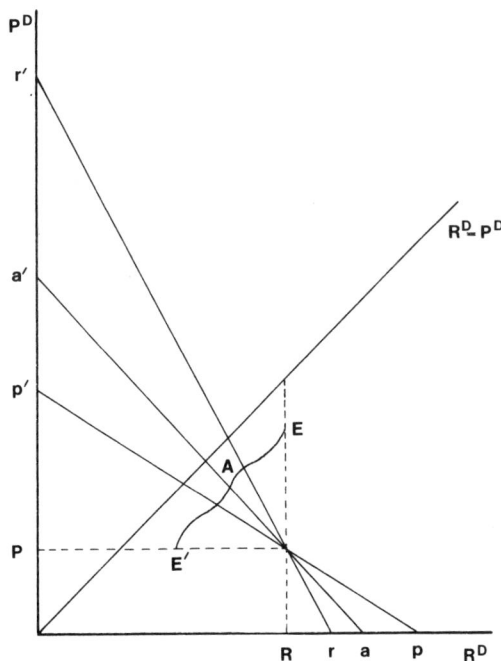

FIGURE 2. *Equilibria as a function of the fraction of the population which is poor.*

dent of n. Thus, there is some lump sum transfer (tax) to a community which will induce it to behave in the same way as any other particular community.

We are now in a position to identify the influence of federal redistributive activity upon local community behavior. We assume initially that the federal government does not allow the deductibility of local taxes nor does it include the local demogrant in taxable income. Thus, a local community's per capita net federal tax payment is

$$t_F \mu(n) - G_F = T_F(n). \tag{8}$$

We require the federal budget to be balanced. Hence

$$\int_0^1 T_F(n) f(n) dn = 0, \tag{9}$$

or

$$t_F \mu(\overline{n}) = G_F, \tag{9'}$$

which combined with (8) yields

$$T_F(n) = t_F [\mu(n) - \mu(\overline{n})]. \tag{8'}$$

Thus, a community's net federal tax (transfer) is a decreasing (increasing) function of n. Moreover, those communities with a poor population below the national mean will pay a positive net federal tax and vice versa. The effect of federal taxes and transfers, then, is to push communities toward A in Figure 2. The poor in richer communities will be made worse off, while those in poor communities are made better off. Thus, federal redistribution is a mixed blessing for the poor. Those in rich states will oppose the expansion of federal redistribution, while those in poor states will support it. Nevertheless, as Figure 2 indicates, federal redistribution reduces disparities between rich and poor overall.

III. OPTIMAL FEDERAL REDISTRIBUTION

Let us turn to the optimization problem confronting the federal government. We assume that the federal government places the same weights upon the rich and poor as the localities. Hence, it seeks to maximize

$$W_F = \int_0^1 W_L(n) f(n) dn, \tag{10}$$

subject to (8) and (9) and individual community behavior.

Income Redistribution in a Federal System

The latter can be summarized by the indirect utility function

$$W_L(n) = V_L(t_F, G_F, n), \tag{11}$$

with

$$\partial V_L / \partial t_F = -\mu(n) U'(P^D) \tag{12}$$

$$\partial V_L / \partial G_F = U'(P^D). \tag{13}$$

The first-order condition for this problem is

$$\int_0^1 U'(P^D, n) [\mu(\overline{n}) - \mu(n)] f(n) dn = 0, \tag{14}$$

or

$$(R - P) \int_0^1 (n - \overline{n}) \{U'(P^D, n) - \overline{U'}\} f(n) dn = 0, \tag{15}$$

where $\overline{U'} = \int U'(P^D, n) f(n) dn$. The left hand side of (15) is proportional to cov $[n, U'(P^D, n)]$. But we have already shown $U'(P^D)$ and n to be positively correlated as long as some communities choose different $\{R^D, P^D\}$. So the optimal solution requires that the federal government set its instruments such that $aU'[R(1 - t_F) + G_F] = U'[P(1 - t_F) + G_F]$. In this case, all communities would choose $t_L = 0$, i.e., the point A in Figure 2. In other words, the orthodox prescription of federal monopolization of the redistributive function is optimal.

IV. DEDUCTIBILITY OF LOCAL TAXES

If local tax payments are deductible from an individual's federal taxes (e.g., $R^D = R(1 - t_L - t_F) + G_L + G_F + t_L t_F R$), it will no longer be optimal for the federal government to monopolize the redistributive function. The first order condition for local governments becomes

$$n(1 - n)(P - R)[aU'(R^D) - U'(P^D)]$$
$$+ t_F[a(1 - n)U'(R^D)R + nU'(P^D)P] = 0 \tag{16}$$

Since the second term in (16) is strictly positive when the federal government redistributes, it follows that $aU'(R^D) > U'(P^D)$. Thus, if the federal government sets its instruments as it did in the previous section, i.e., $aU'(R^D) = U'(P^D)$, local governments will have the incentive to redistribute on their own. In effect, local governments use the federal tax offset to subsidize the cost of local redistributive activity. Federal deductibility amounts to a matching grant for G_L with the federal share equal to its tax rate. Since the federal government can anticipate this local reaction it will choose its instruments so as to keep $[aU'(R^D) - U'(P^D)] > 0$. Some local redistribution, then, will be necessary to achieve the second best solution.

V. REGIONAL COST OF LIVING OR AMENITY DIFFERENTIALS

The local role developed in the preceding section is an artifact of the tax structure and can be eliminated by a suitable tax reform. This would not be the case if there were systematic differences among local communities in the quality of life or the cost of living. Suppose these amenities and living costs are distributed independently of n according to the density function $g(x)$, $\underline{x} \leq x \leq \overline{x}$. Then the federal government's problem is to maximize

$$W_F = \int_{\underline{x}}^{\overline{x}} \int_0^1 W_L(t_F, G_F; n, x) f(n) g(x) dn \, dx \qquad (17)$$

subject to

$$t_F \int_{\underline{x}}^{\overline{x}} \int_0^1 \mu(n, x) f(n) g(x) dn \, dx = G_F. \qquad (18)$$

The first order condition is

$$\int_{\underline{x}}^{\overline{x}} \{(R - P) \, \text{cov}[n, U'(P^D; x, n)] - \overline{n}(x) \, (R - P)$$

$$\int_0^1 [aU'(R^D; x, n) - U'(P^D; x, n)] \, (1 - n) f(n) dn \} g(x) dx$$

$$= 0. \qquad (19)$$

Now if all local governments are at an interior maximum, this reduces to

$$(R - P) \int_{\underline{x}}^{\overline{x}} \text{cov}[n, U'(P^D; x, n)] g(x) dx = 0. \qquad (20)$$

For a given x, the covariance term will be strictly positive unless local governments are preempted by the federal government; i.e.,

Income Redistribution in a Federal System

$$aU'[R(1 - t_F) + G_F; x] - U'[P(1 - t_F) + G_F; x] = 0. \quad (21)$$

Unless the utility function is separable in x, (21) cannot hold for all x. But with (20) being strictly positive, the federal government would attempt to set $t_F = 1$. In this case, however, all local governments cannot be at an interior maximum, for this would require $t_L > 0$ or combined marginal tax rates in excess of 100%. Thus the second term of (19) cannot be zero for all communities.

Now suppose that the federal government chooses (t_F, G_F) such that (21) holds for some amenity level x_0. Suppose further that (21) is increasing in x; i.e., amenities are complementary with high income. Then communities with $x < x_0$ will find it worthwhile to adopt a redistributive tax. However, communities with $x > x_0$ will find (21) to be positive and wish to redistribute income to the rich. But this would require $t_L < 0$, which is ruled out by assumption. Hence communities with relatively high amenities would find themselves at a corner solution.

To summarize, the second term in (19) cannot drop out for all communities because relatively high-amenity localities would find themselves with (21) being positive at $t_L = 0$. Thus, (19) can be written as

$$\int_{\underline{x}}^{x_0} \text{cov }[n, U'(P^D; x)]g(x)dx - \int_{x_0}^{\overline{x}} \overline{n}(x)[1 - \overline{n}(x)]g(x)$$

$$\{aU'[R(1 - t_F) + G_F; x] - U'[P(1 - t_F) + G_F; x]\} dx$$

$$= 0, \quad (22)$$

where the first term is strictly positive and the second term is strictly negative. Hence, the federal government will choose its tax rate such that all communities above some cutoff level of amenities will not choose to augment the federal tax. Among those communities who do redistribute, for given x, those with greater concentrations of poverty will provide smaller redistributive benefits for their poor. On the other hand, for given n, it is those communities with lower amenities who will provide the larger redistributive benefits. It follows that there will be a weak simple correlation between the degree of poverty and the size of local redistributive benefits. This is shown in Figure 3, where local redistributive benefits are denoted as $B_L = P^D - [P(1 - t_F) + G_F]$.

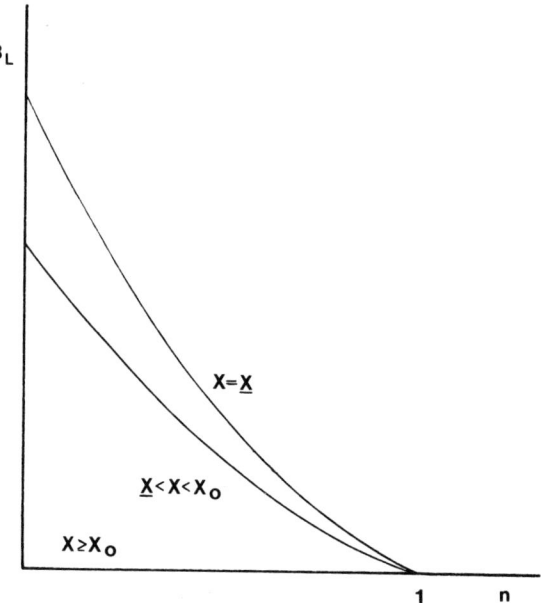

FIGURE 3. *Local redistributive benefits as a function of the fraction of the population which is poor for communities with different levels of amenities.*

VI. TAX AVOIDANCE OR ELASTIC LABOR SUPPLY

We now relax the assumption that taxable income is invariant to the tax rate on income. Instead, we assume that income is made up of two components, one of which is taxable and the other which is not. Let

$$Y = Y_1 + Y_2, \quad Y = R, P, \tag{23}$$

with Y_1 being subject to tax and Y_2 being exempt. The individual is assumed to be able to transform one form of income into the other according to the function

$$H(Y_1, Y_2) - Y = 0, \tag{24}$$

where H is a strictly concave transformation function. The individual maximizes variable income $\tilde{Y}$,

$$\tilde{Y} = Y_1(1 - t_L - t_F) + Y_2 \tag{25}$$

subject to (24). The solution to this problem yields

Income Redistribution in a Federal System

$$Y_1 = h(t_L + t_F), \quad h' < 0, \quad h'' < 0;$$

$$Y_2 = m(t_L + t_F), \quad m' = -(1 - t_F - t_L)h' > 0. \quad (26)$$

Thus, increasing the tax on Y_1 reduces taxable income and increases non-taxable income. The problem of the local government is to choose t_L in order to maximize

$$W_L = nU[h_P(1 - t_L - t_F) + m_P + t_L \mu_1 + G_F]$$
$$+ (1 - n)U[h_R(1 - t_L - t_F) + m_R + t_L \mu_1 + G_F], \quad (27)$$

where $\mu_1 = nh_P + (1-n)h_R$ and $t_L\mu_1 = G_L$. It will be noted that a premium is not attached to the utility of the rich. This device is no longer necessary to prevent full income equality at the local level. Differentiating (27) we obtain

$$\frac{\partial W_L}{\partial t_L} = nU'(P^D)[\mu_1 \varepsilon + (1-n)(h_R - h_P)]$$

$$+ (1-n)U'(R^D)[\mu_1 \varepsilon - n(h_R - h_P)], \quad (28)$$

where

$$\varepsilon = (\partial \mu_1 / \partial t_L)(t_L / \mu_1) \leq 0.$$

Evaluated at $t_L = 0$, (28) becomes

$$\frac{\partial W_L}{\partial t_L} = n(1-n)(h_R - h_P)[U'(P^D) - U'(R^D)], \quad (29)$$

which is positive. Hence all communities will adopt some positive redistribution unless the federal government completely equalizes income. In equilibrium, we have

$$\frac{U'(R^D)}{U'(P^D)} = \frac{[n\mu_1 \varepsilon + n(1-n)(h_R - h_P)]}{[-(1-n)\mu_1 \varepsilon + n(1-n)(h_R - h_P)]} < 1. \quad (30)$$

Because of tax avoidance, the local authorities will not strive for complete income equality; disposable income for the rich will always exceed that for the poor. Hence, our assumption of $a > 1$ in previous sections has some justification.

Moreover, we can totally differentiate (30) to obtain

$$\frac{dR^D}{dn} = \frac{[U'(R^D) - U'(P^D)(dP^D/dR^D)]}{\partial^2 W_L/\partial R^{D2}}, \qquad (31)$$

where dP^D/dR^D is evaluated along the community indifference curves. Since these indifference curves are negatively sloped, the numerator of (31) is strictly positive. Similarly, the denominator of (31) must be negative for the community to be at an interior maximum.[5] Thus, as in our earlier models, redistribution to the poor is negatively correlated with n. It is also easy to show that federal redistributive activity will "crowd out" local redistribution. As in Figure 2, federal redistribution will lead to some of the poor being better off and some worse off.

Let us consider federal redistributive behavior explicitly. Initially, assume that local governments do not act; i.e., $t_L = 0$ for all n. Assuming the federal government maximizes the sum of individual utilities, we obtain

$$\frac{U'(R^D)}{U'(P^D)} = \frac{e_F \overline{Y}_1 \overline{n} + \overline{n}(1-\overline{n})(h_R - h_P)}{-e_F \overline{Y}_1(1-\overline{n}) + \overline{n}(1-\overline{n})(h_R - h_P)} < 1, \qquad (32)$$

where $\overline{n}$ and $\overline{Y}_1$ reflect national averages for the poor population fraction and taxable income and

$$e_F = (d\overline{Y}_1/dt_F)(t_F/\overline{Y}_1) < 0. \qquad (33)$$

In the absence of local redistribution, then, the federal government will not equalize incomes. Furthermore, by (29), every community will seek to augment federal redistribution, with the augmentation greater in the richer communities. If (32) can be considered the optimal distribution for the society, it appears that a federal system will exhibit too much redistribution--quite the opposite of what one has been led to believe. The problem arises because local governments ignore the impact of their activities on federal tax revenues. By raising local taxes, tax avoidance is stimulated with corresponding losses to the federal treasury. Thus, local redistribution carries with it an external diseconomy, leading to excessive redistribution in a federal system. This does not mean that the federal government will not seek to alter its behavior to take the externality into account.

[5]The reader may note that in (31) we have expressed W_L and P^D as functions of R^D, while in (30) they were expressed as functions of t_L. Since we can write R^D as a function of t_L, the treatments are equivalent.

But because of the heterogeneous response to federal tax parameters, the federal government will be unable to obtain a first-best result. The ultimate outcome will be similar to the amenity case, with some local governments redistributing more than others. Unlike the case of amenities, however, all communities will augment federal redistribution.

VII. CONCLUSION

This paper has explored some of the consequences of federalism for the distribution of income in an economy characterized by citizen immobility. Because of differences in resource endowments, local communities can be predicted to differ in the extent to which they engage in redistribution. While federal redistribution will narrow these differentials, it will not eliminate them altogether. Indeed, we have shown that such action may even worsen the plight of some of the poor. We have also shown that the presence of local governments will thwart the efforts of the federal government to achieve a first-best distribution of income. This can result from differences in local environmental public goods or from the failure of local government to internalize the tax avoidance consequences of their fiscal actions. While others have argued that local government redistributive activity will spatially distort resources, distortions will exist even in a world of total immobility.

REFERENCES

Hamilton, B. W., 1975. "Zoning and Property Taxation in a System of Local Governments," *Urban Studies* 12:205-211.
Oakland, W. H., 1979. "Central Cities--Fiscal Plight and Prospects for Reform," in P. Mieszkowski and M. Straszheim (eds.), *Current Issues in Urban Economics*. Baltimore: Johns Hopkins University Press.
Oates, W. E., 1972. *Fiscal Federalism*. New York: Harper, Brace, Jovanovich.
Pauly, M. V., 1973. "Income Redistribution as a Local Public Good," *Journal of Public Economics* 2:35-58.
Tiebout, C. M., 1956. "A Pure Theory of Local Public Expenditures," *Journal of Political Economy* 64:416-424.

Chapter 7

ARE PROPERTY TAXES CAPITALIZED INTO HOUSE VALUES?[1]

Howard S. Bloom
Helen F. Ladd
John Yinger

Program in City and Regional Planning
John F. Kennedy School of Government
Harvard University
Cambridge, Massachusetts

I. INTRODUCTION

What is the effect of property taxes on house values? Theoretically, one would expect houses with higher taxes to have lower values, other things (such as public services, structural characteristics, and neighborhood amenities) being equal. Correspondingly, one would expect a tax increase to reduce house values if nothing else changed.

This phenomenon, generally referred to as property tax capitalization, has important implications for local fiscal policy. It may influence substantially the equity and efficiency of administrative, legislative or judicial decisions that affect property taxes, such as the implementation of tax base sharing, the substitution of state aid for local funds, or the reform of assessment practices. Without capitalization, homeowners could avoid a property tax increase by selling their home. But with capitalization, this avoidance is not possible because the tax increase would be realized as a capital loss upon sale of the house. Correspondingly, with-

―――――――――――
[1] This paper draws on material prepared for the U.S. Department of Housing and Urban Development under Grant H-2915R6. Secretarial assistance was provided by the National Commission for Employment Policy.

out capitalization, households could obtain tax savings by purchasing homes in communities with below average property taxes. But with capitalization, this tax savings would be offset by higher house prices.

Property tax capitalization also has important implications for the theory of local public finance. For example, capitalization is a test of the Tiebout (1956) hypothesis that households choose their residential location at least partly based on local fiscal characteristics. But capitalization may invalidate Tiebout's claim that an optimal distribution of public services is obtainable through a system of independent local jurisdictions.[2]

Theoretical analysis of property tax capitalization dates back to 1735.[3] This theory can be derived in different forms and from different starting points. For example, according to the traditional income approach to property valuation, the value of an asset (in this case a house) equals the discounted present value of its before tax rental stream minus the discounted present value of its tax stream.

Consider a house that provides H units of housing services per year with a before-tax rent of R dollars per year per unit of housing services and a tax payment of T dollars per year. The present value of the corresponding rental stream is RH/r and the present value of the tax stream is T/r, where r is the annual discount rate and the two streams continue in perpetuity.[4] Therefore the value of the house, V, is:

$$V = RH/r - T/r \qquad (1)$$

Equation 1 describes full capitalization, where a house's value is reduced by the full present value of its tax stream.[5] If capitalization is incomplete due to factors such as uncertainty about future taxes, incomplete information about housing market alternatives and Federal income tax deductions for local property taxes, then a house's value is reduced by some fraction, β, of the present value of its tax stream, or:

[2] See Yinger (forthcoming) for a discussion of this issue.
[3] Seligman (1932, pp. 174-175) cites this earliest reference to tax capitalization.
[4] The corresponding n-period present values are obtained by summing $RH/(1 + r)^i$ and $T/(1 + r)^i$ over 1 to n, respectively.
[5] This result can also be derived from a consumer utility maximization problem (see Bloom, Ladd, and Yinger, forthcoming; Yinger, forthcoming).

$$V = RH/r - \beta T/r \tag{2}$$

Equation 2 can be restated in terms of the effective tax rate, t, where t equals T/V, yielding:

$$V = RH/(r + \beta t) \tag{3}$$

To estimate the extent to which capitalization occurs, one must estimate the value of β. A value of β equal to zero indicates that capitalization does not occur and a value of one indicates full or 100 percent capitalization. Results between these two extremes represent partial capitalization.

For example, consider two identical houses where $R1 = R2$ and $H1 = H2$. Assume the market value of the first house, $V1$, exceeds the market value of the second house, $V2$, by \$1,000 and the present value of the tax stream for the first house, $T1/r$, is \$2,000 less than the present value of the tax stream for the second house, $T2/r$. Then:

$$\begin{aligned} V1 - V2 &= (R1H1/r - \beta T1/r) - (R2H2/r - \beta T2/r) \\ &= -\beta (T1/r - T2/r) \\ &= \$1000 \end{aligned} \tag{4}$$

and

$$T1/r - T2/r = -\$2000 \tag{5}$$

Thus

$$\frac{-\beta (T1/r - T2/r)}{(T1/r - T2/r)} = \frac{1000}{-2000} \tag{6}$$

or

$$\beta = 0.5 \tag{7}$$

House values are reduced by half the present value of property taxes, representing 50 percent capitalization.

In this paper we review the empirical property tax capitalization literature to obtain the best possible estimate of β. This literature consists of three parts: (1) studies based on average house values and related aggregate data for local jurisdictions; (2) studies based on cross-sectional micro-data from the sale of individual houses; and (3) studies based on micro-data describing changes in the taxes and values of individual homes. The studies considered are listed in Table I.

TABLE I. Empirical Property Tax Capitalization Studies

Studies Based on Aggregate Data	Studies Based on Cross-Sectional Micro-Data	Studies Based on Micro-Data Describing Tax Changes
Oates (1969, 1973)	King (1973)	Wicks, Little, and Beck (1968)
Heinberg and Oates (1970)	Church (1974)	Smith (1970)
Pollakowski (1973)	Wales and Weins (1974)	Moody (1974)
Edel and Sclar (1974)	Edelstein (1974)	Bloom, Ladd, and Yinger
Gustely (1976)	Case (1978)	(forthcoming)
Meadows (1976)	Hamilton (1979)	
McDougall (1976)		
King (1977)		
Rosen and Fullerton (1977)		

To interpret the results of these studies, it is useful to keep two distinctions in mind. First one should distinguish between effects of taxes with and without the corresponding effects of local public services. We focus on tax effects, holding services constant. A second distinction is the difference between: (1) capitalization of interjurisdictional tax differences, due for example to differences in tax bases, access to state and Federal aid, or costs of providing public services; and (2) capitalization of intrajurisdictional tax differences, due largely to imperfect assessment practices. We examine both types of capitalization.

Two key results emerge from our literature review. First, although the theory of property tax capitalization is straightforward, we find that it is extremely difficult to estimate the extent to which capitalization occurs. Foremost among the problems facing researchers are: (1) simultaneity bias due to reciprocal causality between house values and property taxes; (2) left-out-variable bias due to the inability to control for all house value determinants that are correlated with property taxes; and (3) difficulties determining an appropriate discount rate.

Our second finding is that, despite these problems, the empirical capitalization literature presents a cumulative body of evidence indicating a substantial degree of property tax capitalization. This result holds for both interjurisdictional and intrajurisdictional tax capitalization.

In the following sections, we review each of the major types of capitalization studies, summarizing their findings, describing their methodologies and examining their strengths and weaknesses. We do not consider studies of the relationship between taxes and rents (e.g., Orr, 1968; Hyman and Pasour, 1973) because they only provide indirect information about capitalization and involve issues well beyond the scope of this paper.[6]

II. STUDIES BASED ON AGGREGATE DATA

A. Findings

Aggregate capitalization studies observe the relationship between interjurisdictional variations in average property taxes and corresponding variations in average house values,

[6] We also do not consider very early tax capitalization studies (Jensen, 1931; Daicoff, 1962; Woodard and Brady, 1965), given the methodological advances that have been made since these studies were published.

controlling for other house value determinants. Most of these studies are extensions of Oates' 1969 seminal work using data for 53 New Jersey communities to estimate the effect of property taxes and local public expenditures on median house values. Oates found 65 percent tax capitalization (using a 5 percent discount rate) and evidence consistent with the capitalization of public school expenditures. In addition, he found that school expenditures almost completely offset the effect of taxes used to finance them. Later, in response to criticism of his work (Pollakowski, 1973), Oates (1973) modified his model and obtained 90 percent capitalization.

Findings from the aggregate literature range from 100 percent tax capitalization (Heinberg and Oates, 1970) to no capitalization (Pollakowski, 1973), although most studies find between 40 percent and 90 percent capitalization (Oates, 1969, 1973; McDougall, 1976; King, 1977; and Rosen and Fullerton, 1977).

B. Analysis

Aggregate property tax capitalization studies are based on regression models specifying that house values depend on property taxes, public services, structural characteristics, neighborhood characteristics, and accessibility to employment. For example, Oates based his final conclusions on a regression model of median house values as a function of effective tax rates, school expenditures per pupil, nonschool expenditures per capita, median rooms per house, and distance from midtown Manhattan.[7]

The degree to which property taxes are capitalized (the value of in our earlier theoretical discussion) can be estimated by comparing the regression's prediction for the impact of a tax change with the impact implied by full capitalization. For example, the tax rate coefficient obtained by Oates implies that increasing the effective property tax rate from 2 percent to 3 percent decreases house values by $2,030. But full capitalization implies a $2,500 reduction for Oates' example of a $20,000 house and a 5 percent discount rate. Hence the estimate degree of capitalization is $2,030/$2,500 or 81 percent.[8]

[7] See Oates (1973), p. 1006.
[8] The difference between the 81 percent capitalization figure in this example and the 90 percent figure obtained from Oates' computation is the fact that he assumes a forty year lifetime for the house, and we use formulas for an infinite lifetime.

C. *Methodological Problems*

Findings from the aggregate capitalization literature must be interpreted with caution because of the unresolved methodological problems described in the following five subsections.

1. Simultaneity Bias. All authors except King (1977) use average effective tax rate as their independent tax variable. But this variable is approximately equal to the average tax payment divided by the average house value. Thus house values negatively affect tax rates, creating simultaneity bias which causes one to overestimate the negative capitalization effect of taxes on values.

Beginning with Oates, authors have recognized this problem and have attempted to eliminate it by using two-stage least squares. But as Pollakowski (1973) indicates, the results of this procedure are highly sensitive to model specification. He contends that Oates' use of two-stage least squares does not fully purge his capitalization estimates of simultaneity bias because his first-stage independent variables are related to the error term in the second-stage house value equation. By using these variables in the first stage to predict second-stage values for property taxes, Oates builds in, rather than eliminates simultaneity bias. To avoid this problem one needs a strong theoretical base for specifying both the first and second-stage equations--a base which no study has yet fully attained.

2. Left-Out-Variable Bias. Unbiased estimates of tax capitalization require that all house value determinants correlated with taxes be included in one's regression model. Otherwise capitalization estimates are subject to left-out-variable bias.[9]

Identifying and measuring all necessary variables is difficult even when using micro-data sets (to be described later) with detailed house characteristics. But aggregate studies typically use only a few such control variables. For example, Oates (1969, 1973), Heinberg and Oates (1970), Meadows (1976), Rosen and Fullerton (1977), and King (1977) use building age and rooms per unit to represent structural characteristics and income and accessibility to represent neighborhood characteristics. Similarly, Edel and Sclar

---

[9]*It is also theoretically possible to obtain unbiased tax capitalization estimates if the biases of different left-out variables neutralize each other.*

(1974) use density and percent of dwellings owner-occupied. And when re-estimating Oates' model, Pollakowski (1973) uses only building age, rooms per unit, and accessibility.

3. *Problems with the Tax Variable.* There are three major problems with the tax variable used by most aggregate capitalization studies. The first problem was noted by King (1977). Most authors specify house value models that imply that a given change in the tax rate affects all house values equally. But since the tax payment associated with a given tax rate change depends on the value of the house, this specification is incorrect. The direction of the resulting bias is not obvious, however, although King contends that this misspecification causes Oates (1973) to overestimate tax capitalization by about 40 percent.[10]

A second problem with the effective tax rate variable is measurement error. This is particularly troublesome for Gustely (1976) and Meadows (1976) who use equalized tax rate data. These data are based on official equalized tax base estimates which are often inaccurate because of the small and sparsely reported samples of house sales upon which they are based. Furthermore, equalized property values are sometimes subject to negotiation because they form the basis for distributing state aid.

The third tax variable problem applies only to Edel and Sclar's 1974 study of Massachusetts communities. They use nominal, instead of effective, tax rates for all years except 1970, for which they replicate their analysis using both tax rates. Since nominal tax rates apply to assessed rather than market values and assessment-sales ratios vary dramatically across communities in Massachusetts, nominal tax rates are poor, indeed virtually meaningless, indicators of relative tax burdens across communities.

4. *Problems Measuring Public Service Levels.* Several authors emphasize the importance of accurately measuring public service levels. These measures affect estimates of public service capitalization. But they also affect estimates of tax capitalization because of their correlation with both house values and property taxes. Two problems arise when attempting to measure public service levels: (1) deciding which services to include and (2) deciding how to measure the level of each service.

Oates uses public education in his model and measures service levels by expenditures per pupil. In response to criticism from Pollakowski (1973), Oates (1973) added total nonschool expenditures per capita. This increased his esti-

---

[10]*See King (1977), p. 430.*

mate of tax capitalization from 65 percent to 90 percent. Later studies consider expenditures for a variety of services (total nonschool expenditures per capita (Meadows, 1976; Gustely, 1976) and highway maintenance expenditures per square mile (Edel and Sclar, 1974)). Rosen and Fullerton (1977) extend Oates' work by measuring school output by fourth grade test scores. They find 88 percent tax capitalization using test scores as compared to 75 percent using per-pupil school expenditures. McDougall (1976) includes twelfth grade test scores, crime rates, fire insurance ratings, and a recreational quality index. On balance, it appears that inclusion of more services makes a greater difference for tax capitalization estimates than does refinement of the measures used for each service.

5. *Selection of a Discount Rate.* As explained earlier, to convert regression coefficients into estimates of the degree to which taxes are capitalized requires an assumption about the discount rate. Oates (1969, 1973), Heinberg and Oates (1970), King (1977), and McDougall (1976) use 5 percent, Rosen and Fullerton (1977) use 6 percent, and Edel and Sclar (1974) use 8 percent.

Selection of an appropriate discount rate raises complex issues that have been discussed widely. In particular one must account for likely future inflation rates and changes in the real rate of interest. Thus studies based on data from different periods may need to use different discount rates. But choosing a rate is quite difficult.

Unfortunately, estimates of the degree to which capitalization occurs are sensitive to the discount rate which is assumed. In the numerical example discussed earlier, if we had assumed an 8 percent discount rate instead of a five percent rate, we would have obtained 111 percent instead of 81 percent capitalization. This problem also applies to all but one of the studies based on micro-data discussed in the following sections.

III. STUDIES BASED ON CROSS-SECTIONAL MICRO-DATA

A. *Findings*

Because studies using cross-sectional micro-data are based on large samples (containing up to 2195 observations, Case (1978)) with many detailed housing characteristics (up to 90, Church (1974)), left-out-variable bias is probably not a major problem. Furthermore, these studies add a new dimension to the analysis of property tax capitalization by examining the effect of intrajurisdictional tax differences (King, 1973; Church, 1974; Edelstein, 1974; Wales and Weins, 1974; Case, 1978; Hamilton, 1979) as well as interjurisdictional tax differences (King, 1973; Edelstein, 1974; Case, 1978; Hamilton, 1979).

In addition, these studies have at least two other important strengths. First they can measure property taxes more accurately than is possible using existing aggregate data. Tax payment estimates can be obtained from available information on nominal tax rates and assessed values for each house. And effective tax rates can be obtained by dividing tax payments by observed sales prices. Second, studies based on data from the sale of individual house control for variations in public service levels to a greater extent than is possible using existing aggregate data because public services vary more across than within jurisdictions.

On balance these studies find substantial capitalization of both interjurisdictional and intrajurisdictional property tax variations. The only study in this group that does not find capitalization, Wales and Weins (1974), is subject to methodological problems that make interpretation of its findings extremely difficult. Most estimates for both types of capitalization are within the 40 to 90 percent range obtained from the aggregate capitalization literature. This range is disappointingly large, but the consistency of evidence with respect to the existence of property tax capitalization is impressive.

B. Analysis and Methodological Problems

Studies in this group use data for individual house sales to estimate regression models of the following form:

$$V = \alpha + \beta \cdot TAX + \sum_j \delta_j \cdot X_j + \varepsilon \tag{8}$$

where:

V = house value (sales price);

TAX = a property tax variable--either property tax payment, T, or property tax rate, t;

X_j = the jth house characteristic such as the public service level or number of rooms; and

ε = a random error term.

Studies that examine only intrajurisdictional tax capitalization estimate models from a sample of house sales located in a single jurisdiction. Case (1978) uses 1084 house sales from Hanford, California during the period 1972 to 1975; Wales and Weins (1974) use 1828 house sales from Surrey, British Columbia in 1972; and Church (1974) uses 957 house sales from Martinez, California during the period 1967-1970.

Other authors examine both intrajurisdictional and interjurisdictional tax capitalization by estimating models for house sales from several jurisdictions. Case (1978) uses 2195 house sales from 13 Boston area communities in 1971; King (1973) uses 1892 house sales from 10 New Haven area municipalities during the period 1967 to 1969; and Edelstein (1974) uses 2143 house sales from six suburban Philadelphia townships during the period 1967 to 1969. To control for public service variations across jurisdictions, Case (1978) uses per-pupil school expenditures and dummy variables; King (1973) uses a variety of objective and subjective public service measures; Edelstein (1974) uses dummy variables to identify different communities; and Hamilton (1979) uses a measure of net benefits from the tax-service package.[11]

As previously indicated, all but one of these studies finds substantial property tax capitalization. This result does not depend on a particular model or type of data. Nevertheless each study has its own strengths and weaknesses, a detailed discussion of which is beyond the scope of this paper. Readers who wish to further examine these studies should pay particular attention to the manner in which they: (1) deal with the simultaneity bias; (2) specify the property tax variable; (3) control for structural characteristics, neighborhood factors and public services; and (4) determine a discount rate.

The only study in this group that does not find capitalization, Wales and Weins (1974), requires further explanation. Wales and Weins begin by focusing on two major methodological problems, simultaneity bias and misspecification of the tax variable. Simultaneity bias arises when the tax variable in Equation 8 is the effective tax rate. The effective tax rate equals the annual tax payment divided by house value. Thus holding the tax payment constant, an increase in house value decreases the effective tax rate, producing negative simultaneity bias in estimates of the tax rate coefficient.

The second problem arises if one takes King's advice (1977) and uses tax payments instead of effective tax rates.

---

[11] *Hamilton's (1979) approach raises questions about the way to value public services that are beyond the scope of this paper.*

Tax payments equal the nominal tax rate established by each jurisdiction times the assessed value of each house. But assessed values are in part a function of market value, which produces a positive simultaneity bias in estimates of the coefficient for the tax variable.

Wales and Weins attempt to eliminate simultaneity bias in capitalization estimates based on tax rates by using a Monte Carlo simulation. They first ignore the simultaneity and estimate Equation 8, obtaining a negative and statistically significant value for β. Because this estimate contains a negative simultaneity bias it overestimates tax capitalization. To estimate the magnitude of this bias, the authors drop the tax rate variable and estimate the following regression:

$$V = \alpha' + \sum_j \delta'_j X_j + \varepsilon' \tag{9}$$

They use the resulting coefficients to create a new variable.

$$\hat{V} = \hat{\alpha}' + \sum_j \hat{\delta}'_j X_j \tag{10}$$

Then they add a random component to $\hat{V}$ by drawing a random variable, u, from a distribution with a standard deviation equal to the standard error of Equation 9 creating:

$$\tilde{V} = \hat{V} + u \tag{11}$$

In a world with no capitalization, a regression of house values on tax rates and house characteristics should yield a β of zero, except to the extent that simultaneity biases this estimate downward. Thus using their simulated data-set to estimate β''' from the following regression:

$$\tilde{V} = \alpha'' + \beta'' t + \sum_j \delta''_j X_j + \varepsilon'', \tag{12}$$

the authors claim to obtain a direct estimate of simultaneity bias. They subtract this estimate of the bias (from Equation 12) from their biased estimate of β (from Equation 8) to obtain a presumably unbiased estimate of β. Since this difference is very close to zero they suggest that property taxes are not capitalized.

If, in fact, there is no capitalization, their procedure is correct. But if there is capitalization, their procedure may become circular. If capitalization exists (i.e., $\beta \neq 0$) and t is correlated with the X_j's the $\hat{\delta}'_j$ will incorporate some of the effect of variation in t. Hence $\hat{V}$ and thus $\tilde{V}$ will contain a component due to t. When estimating Equation 12 from the simulated data, this component is attributed to β'' (as it should be) and thus the simulated results contain estimates of both true capitalization and simultaneity bias. Therefore, the estimated coefficient, $\hat{\beta}''$, is not a good measure of simultaneity bias. Because estimates of β from the original and simulated data sets contain the same two components (capitalization and simultaneity bias), it is not surprising that they are virtually identical.

IV. STUDIES BASED ON MICRO-DATA REPRESENTING TAX CHANGES

The last four studies to be discussed, Wicks, Little, and Beck (1968), Smith (1970), Moody (1974), and Bloom, Ladd, and Yinger (forthcoming) present consistent evidence of property tax capitalization. Three of these studies deal with intrajurisdictional capitalization and one deals with interjurisdictional capitalization. All four studies are based on individual house sales. But what distinguishes them from the preceding studies is their attempt to observe the response of house values to institutional changes that alter property taxes.

Wicks, Little, and Beck (1968) and Smith (1970) use tax changes generated by jurisdiction-wide reassessments. Because assessment-sales ratios, and thus effective tax rates, typically vary widely within a jurisdiction, reassessment to a uniform effective tax rate shifts taxes dramatically--often by several hundred percent. Using 64 house sales from Missoula, Montana in 1965 and 301 house sales from San Francisco during the period 1966 to 1968, Wicks, Little, and Beck (1968) and Smith (1970) respectively, compare the change in tax payment, T, for each house with the difference between what the house sold for, V, and an estimate of what it would have sold for if taxes had not been changed V'. Both authors find substantial capitalization, *i.e.*, the difference between observed and forecasted house values (sales prices) increased as the change in taxes generated by reassessment increased.

Wicks, Little, and Beck (1968) report an average capitalization ratio of 19, which indicates a $19 decrease in value for each $1 annual increase in taxes, despite a bias against observing capitalization caused by the way they predict house values without the tax shift. This bias arises from their use of the following relationship:

$$V' = Al(\overline{SARI})I \qquad (13)$$

where V' = the predicted market value without the tax shift; Al = the assessed value before reassessment; $(\overline{SARI})$ = the mean sales/assessment ratio prior to reassessment; and I = a housing price index. Note that the tax change, ΔT, increases, on average, as $(SAR1)$, the actual pre-assessment sales/assessment ratio for a particular house, decreases. Consequently, $(\overline{SAR1})$ is a greater underestimate of $(SAR1)$ and V' is a greater underestimate of V, as ΔT increases. Thus $(V-V')$ is overestimated by more as T increases. This error will lead to an underestimate of capitalization.

Smith (1970) obtains an average capitalization ratio of 14.5. In addition, because he uses sales data for the period starting before reassessment was announced and ending after it was fully implemented, he observes capitalization of anticipated tax changes.

Moody (1974) uses a simple but clever approach. From sales data for 518 similar houses on both sides of the boundary between San Francisco and Daly City, California, he observes the response of house values to a decision in 1963 to construct a Bay Area Rapid Transit station at this boundary. Average sales prices rose dramatically on both sides of the boundary following this decision. But they rose by less on the San Francisco side where residents had to pay an additional property tax to support construction of the transit system. Moody attributes this difference to property tax capitalization.

More precisely, he proceeds as follows. Using data for the sale of houses before 1963, he computes separate house value trends for San Francisco and Daly City. Then using post-1963 sales data he computes the deviation (in this case positive) of average house prices in each city from expected house prices forecasted by the price trend for that city. The difference between San Francisco's deviation from its trend and Daly City's deviation from its trend ranges from $285 to $478 depending upon the model used for the analysis. Moody prefers the $285 figure based on results of several statistical tests. He compares this $285 differential to the $13 to $16 average annual transit-related property tax differential between the two cities to compute measures of the extent to which taxes are capitalized.

To interpret results of the preceding three studies one must select an appropriate discount rate. For example, given a 5 percent rate, Wicks, Little, and Beck (1968) obtain 95 percent capitalization, Smith (1970) obtains 73 percent capitalization and Moody's (1974) preferred result implies from 89 to 109 percent capitalization. With an 8 percent discount rate these estimates become 152 percent, 116 percent, and 142 to 174 percent capitalization.

The most recent study included in this review is an analysis of intrajurisdictional property tax capitalization by Bloom, Ladd, and Yinger (forthcoming). The authors base their analysis on tax changes generated by jurisdiction-wide reassessments in seven Boston area municipalities during 1967-1974. Within each municipality they collect data for all houses that sold more than once during a period beginning five years before reassessment and ending five years after reassessment. Of particular interest are houses that sold both before and after reassessment, because property taxes for many of these houses changed dramatically. By collecting sales price (market value) and property tax information for these "double sales" the authors observe directly the response of house values to property tax changes.

Using samples ranging from 188 to 556 "double sales," the authors replicate their analysis for each municipality in their sample. Due in large part to differences in data availability and quality, their most defensible tax capitalization estimates range from 40 to 90 percent. Their single best estimate (*i.e.*, that based on the most complete data) is 90 percent.

The statistical model used by the authors is similar to Equation 3 stated in difference form. The functional form for the model is derived theoretically to reduce the likelihood of specification error. To eliminate community-wide housing inflation over time, the authors deflate all sales prices by a housing price index developed by Bailey, Muth, and Nourse (1963) and estimated separately from double sales data for each municipality. In addition, they employ a set of variables that identify the timing of the first and second sale of each "double sale" to eliminate the effect of interjurisdiction changes over time in relative property tax rates. This isolates the effect of intrajurisdictional tax rate changes.

For two of their seven jurisdictions, detailed house characteristics were available from the local assessor and neighborhood characteristics were obtained from the 1970 U.S. Census. Thus there was a high degree of control (both through the "double sale" methodology and through statistical methods based on the additional data that were collected) for housing and neighborhood characteristics. Furthermore by obtaining data for houses that sold before, during, and after the announcement and implementation of reassessment, the authors were able to distinguish between the capitalization of anticipated and realized changes in property taxes. Between the announcement and implementation of reassessment there was a noticeable capitalization of likely future tax changes, which was smaller in magnitude than the ultimate capitalization of actual tax changes.

Last, and perhaps most important, is the authors' treatment of the two most serious problems affecting previous capitalization studies: simultaneity bias and the need to assume a discount rate.

Their house value model is based on effective tax rates which, as indicated previously, have a negative reciprocal linkage to house values. To minimize simultaneity bias due to this linkage, the authors use two-stage least squares, emphasizing the development of a theoretically derived specification for the first-stage regression to reduce the chances of using independent variables which are correlated with the error term in the second-stage house value equation.

The authors eliminate the need to assume a discount rate by specifying this rate as an estimable parameter in their model. They estimate this parameter simultaneously with all others in the model using an iterative nonlinear least squares procedure.

V. CONCLUSIONS AND SUGGESTED FURTHER RESEARCH

A. *Conclusions*

Existing empirical evidence, although subject to serious methodological problems, strongly suggests a substantial degree of both interjurisdictional and intrajurisdictional property tax capitalization. This conclusion is based on findings obtained from a broad array of estimation procedures and reflects conditions in many different locations and time periods.

Evidence about interjurisdictional capitalization comes from aggregate cross-sectional studies based on data from the sale of individual houses, and a unique analysis of the effect of a major public service/tax decision. Assuming a five percent discount rate, these studies represent 100, 99, 90, 73, 67, 50, 45, and 35 percent capitalization (Heinberg and Oates, 1970; Moody, 1974; Oates, 1973; Rosen and Fullerton, 1977; King, 1977; McDougall, 1976; Case, 1978; King, 1973). Assuming an 8 percent discount rate these estimates become 160, 158, 144, 117, 107, 80, 71, and 50 percent, respectively. During the period represented by these results, mortgage interest rates were between five and eight percent.[12] However, studies yielding above 100 percent capitalization at the assumed 8 percent discount rate represent the early part of this period when mortgage rates were between five and six percent. Thus we conclude that inter-

[12]Economic Report of the President (1980), *p. 278.*

jurisdictional property tax variations are between halfway and fully capitalized into house values. Note, that in addition to the preceding studies, others whose numerical results cannot be summarized readily (Edel and Sclar, 1974; Gustely, 1976; Meadows, 1976; Edelstein, 1974; Hamilton, 1979) provide consistent evidence of interjurisdictional property tax capitalization.

Evidence about intrajurisdictional tax capitalization comes primarily from studies of the impact on individual house values of tax changes caused by jurisdiction-wide reassessment. Assuming a five percent discount rate, Wicks, Little, and Beck (1968) find 95 percent intrajurisdictional tax capitalization and Smith (1970) finds 73 percent. Assuming an eight percent discount rate (which is well above mortgage interest rates during the period represented by their studies) these figures become 152 percent and 116 percent respectively. Without having to assume a discount rate, Bloom, Ladd, and Yinger (forthcoming) find between 40 and 90 percent capitalization, with a single best estimate of 90 percent. Therefore we conclude that intrajurisdictional *changes* in property taxes are between halfway and fully capitalized into house values.

B. Suggested Further Research

Where should we go from here? First, serious methodological problems remain to be solved before conclusive evidence of capitalization can be obtained. Because of simultaneity bias, left-out variable bias and the need to assume a discount rate, the evidence to date is highly suggestive but not conclusive.

Second, it is likely that property tax capitalization varies due to factors such as the degree of uncertainty about future property taxes, the type of housing market (e.g., loose versus tight and urban versus rural), the level of and general concern about property taxes, and the marginal Federal income tax rate. Research into the determinants of the extent to which property taxes are capitalized thus should be encouraged.

Lastly, but perhaps most importantly, we need more research on the theoretical and practical implications of property tax capitalization. For example, Yinger (forthcoming) illustrates how the capitalization of property taxes and local public services produces inefficiency in a Tiebout (1956) model. And Bloom, Ladd, and Yinger (forthcoming) demonstrate how local assessors can use capitalization estimates when they reassess property to account for the effect of the tax changes caused by their reassessment.

REFERENCES

Bailey, M. J., R. F. Muth, and H. O. Nourse, 1963. "A Regression Model for Real Estate Price Index Construction," *Journal of the American Statistical Association* 58:469-482.

Bloom, H. S., H. F. Ladd, and J. Yinger, forthcoming. *Property Taxes and House Values*. New York: Academic Press.

Case, C. E., 1978. *Property Taxation: The Need for Reform*. Cambridge, Massachusetts: Ballinger.

Church, A. M., 1974. "Capitalization of the Effective Property Tax Rate on Single Family Homes," *National Tax Journal* 28:113-122.

Daicoff, D. W., 1962. *Capitalization of the Property Tax*, Ph. D. Dissertation, Department of Economics, University of Michigan.

Economic Report of the President 1980, Washington, D.C.: U.S. Government Printing Office.

Edel, M., and E. Sclar, 1974. "Taxes, Spending and Property Values: Supply Adjustment in a Tiebout-Oates Model," *Journal of Political Economy* 82:941-954.

Edelstein, R., 1974. "The Determinants of Value in the Philadelphia Housing Market: A Case Study of the Main Line 1967-1969," *The Review of Economics and Statistics* 56:319-327.

Gustely, D., 1976. "Local Taxes, Expenditures and Urban Housing: A Reassessment of the Evidence," *Southern Economic Journal* 42:659-665.

Hamilton, B. W., 1979. "Capitalization and the Regressivity of the Property Tax: Empirical Evidence," *National Tax Journal*, Supplement, June 1979, 169-180.

Heinberg, J. D., and W. E. Oates, 1970. "The Incidence of Differential Property Taxes on Urban Housing: A Comment and Some Further Evidence," *National Tax Journal* 23:92-98.

Hyman, D., and E. C. Pasour, 1973. "Property Tax Differentials and Residential Rents in North Carolina," *National Tax Journal* 26:303-307.

Jensen, J. P., 1931. *Property Taxation in the United States*. Chicago: The University of Chicago Press.

King, A. T., 1973. *Property Taxes, Amenities and Residential Land Values*. Cambridge, Massachusetts: Ballinger.

King, A. T., 1977. "Estimating Property Tax Capitalization: A Critical Comment," *Journal of Political Economy* 85:425-431.

McDougall, G. A., 1976. "Local Public Goods and Residential Property Values: Some Insights and Extensions," *National Tax Journal* 29:436-447.

Meadows, G. R., 1976. "Taxes, Spending and Property Values: A Comment and Further Results," *Journal of Political Economy* 84:869-880.

Moody, J. P., 1974. *Testing Tax Capitalization: An Experiment Afforded by a Local Public Transit Improvement*, Department of Economics, University of California, Berkeley.

Oates, W. E., 1969. "The Effects of Property Taxes and Local Spending on Property Values: An Empirical Study of Tax Capitalization and the Tiebout Hypothesis," *Journal of Political Economy* 77:957-971.

Oates, W. E., 1973. "The Effects of Property Taxes and Local Public Spending on Property Values: A Reply and Yet Further Results," *Journal of Political Economy* 81:1004-1008.

Orr, L. L., 1968. "The Incidence of Differential Property Taxes on Urban Housing," *National Tax Journal* 21:253-262.

Pollakowski, H. E., 1973. "The Effects of Property Taxes and Local Public Spending on Property Values: A Comment and Further Results," *Journal of Political Economy* 81:994-1003.

Rosen, H. S., and D. J. Fullerton, 1977. "A Note on Local Tax Rates, Public Benefit Levels and Property Values," *Journal of Political Economy* 85:433-440.

Seligman, E. R., 1932. *The Shifting and Incidence of Taxation*, 5th Edition, New York: Columbia University Press.

Smith, A. S., 1970. "Property Tax Capitalization in San Francisco," *National Tax Journal* 23:177-193.

Tiebout, C. M., 1956. "A Pure Theory of Local Expenditures," *Journal of Political Economy* 64:416-424.

Wales, T. J., and E. G. Weins, 1974. "Capitalization of Residential Property Taxes: An Empirical Study," *Review of Economics and Statistics* 56:329-333.

Wicks, J. H., R. A. Little, and R. A. Beck, 1968. "A Note on Capitalization of Property Tax Changes," *National Tax Journal* 21:263-265.

Woodard, F. O., and R. W. Brady, 1965. "Inductive Evidence of Tax Capitalization," *National Tax Journal* 18:193-201.

Yinger, J., forthcoming. "Capitalization and the Theory of Local Public Finance," *Journal of Political Economy*.

Chapter 8

VOTING AND SPENDING: SOME EMPIRICAL
RELATIONSHIPS IN THE POLITICAL ECONOMY
OF LOCAL PUBLIC FINANCE[1]

Thomas Romer
Howard Rosenthal

Graduate School of Industrial Administration
Carnegie-Mellon University
Pittsburgh, Pennsylvania

I. INTRODUCTION

How does the political structure of decision making affect local public spending? Is the bureaucracy associated with the provision of local public goods able to exert monopoly power? Do competitive political pressures, perhaps enhanced by voter mobility, mitigate the possibility for spending in excess of that desired by some "median voter"? The answers to these questions involve considerations of both political and economic forces. In this paper, we summarize our current empirical examination of these issues in the context of local expenditure determination by direct democracy. The major intent of the paper is to present what appear to be fairly robust "stylized facts." We offer a theoretical basis for some of these observed regularities. (In fact, we looked for them because of theoretical predictions.) Others we present for purposes of discussion and to motivate further research. The empirical focus is Oregon school districts from 1970 through 1976.

[1]This research was supported by National Science Foundation grant DAR79-17576. The Spencer Foundation provided earlier support for data collection and processing. We thank George Zodrow for excellent editorial comments and Krishna Ladha for research assistance.

A. *Spending Under Full Information Conditions*

Our initial work (Romer and Rosenthal, 1978) was developed in a framework where all citizens had full information about voter preferences and where the behavior of voters could be predicted with certainty. Motivated by the work of Niskanen (1971), we analyzed a model where a budget-maximizing agenda setter confronted the electorate with a forced choice between a proposed budget and an exogenously imposed reversion level. The reversion is the amount of spending that would occur if the setter's proposal were rejected by half or more of the voters. In this model, expenditure decreases as the reversion approaches the median voter's ideal point from below, and equals the reversion for reversions at or above the median ideal point. Unless the reversion exactly equals the median ideal point, expenditures always exceed the median ideal point.

The reversion, in Oregon, is highly unlikely to approximate the median ideal point. In part, the reversion consists of lump-sum intergovernmental transfers that are not contingent on the voters approving the budget. These account only for about half of total expenditures. The other component of the reversion is a constitutionally defined base amount, augmented annually at six percent in nominal terms, and varying from zero, in many districts, to over $50,000,000 in Portland. Thus, a finding that districts spent exactly their reversion would, except by chance, run counter to the standard median voter model.

B. *Uncertainty*

Later theoretical work (Romer and Rosenthal, 1979) introduced uncertainty. Individual voter turnout was modeled as a process that was random but independent of both the reversion and the setter's proposal. Even this very simple form of uncertainty destroys the neat functional dependence found in the full information story. We know only that (a) for reversions at or above the median ideal point, both the actual and the expected budget under uncertainty equal or exceed the certainty budget; (b) for very low reversions, the expected budget under uncertainty is less than the certainty budget. Otherwise, the expected budget can be either increasing or decreasing in the reversion and may indeed fall below the median ideal point, even if the setter is risk-neutral. While the relationship between reversions and spending may be complex, the setter model predicts that reversions are statistically important in explaining spending.

Empirically, we modeled this relationship as one in which there was a threshold level. Reversions below this level meant funds insufficient to operate the schools. This would act as a threat to voters, and expenditures could be expected to be substantially greater for reversions just below the threshold than for reversions just above it. Above the threshold, we allowed for a log-linear relationship between the spending and the reversion.

In our empirical work, we have confronted the setter model and the median voter model in a variety of ways. First, we showed that districts failing to hold elections spent virtually 100 percent of their reversion. Since a budget-maximizer will never spend less than the reversion, this outcome is consistent with the setter model. On the other hand, as indicated above, spending exactly the reversion is highly unlikely under the median voter story.[2] Second, we examined special elections to modify the reversion. This provided evidence strongly in favor of the setter model. The major points are (a) that the proposed new reversion was almost always for an amount in excess of current spending levels (again the proposal is controlled by the setter, who is made worse off by increased reversions that are below current spending); (b) that such proposals almost always failed (note that the median voter would, in a static world, reject new reversions above current spending); and (c) that such proposals occur very rarely (the setter should realize his proposed new reversion will not pass). Third, we estimated an expenditure model that disclosed significant reversion effects, with the threshold effect estimated to increase spending by 15 percent.

In the course of estimating the expenditure model, we experimented by considering a specification which supposed that state aid is not perceived by the voters. (State aid is approximately one-fourth of total operating expenses, consisting nearly entirely of lump-sum grants.) We defined perceived spending as true spending less state aid and the perceived reversion as the true reversion less state aid. We obtained significantly "better" estimates with this specification. This result and the result that the reversion effect was clearly inconsistent with a full information model led us to conclude that future research should address the essential questions of perception and information. These questions are

---

[2]*See Romer and Rosenthal (1979). The remainder of this paragraph and all of the next summarizes Romer and Rosenthal (forthcoming-b).*

prominent in the traditional political science literature but are largely ignored in the formal literature on voting, social choice, and local public goods.[3]

We pursue these matters in the present paper. In Section II, we discuss perception of intergovernmental aid in the expenditure equation. In Section III, we discuss cuts in proposed per student spending following voter rejection of a previous budget proposal. In Section IV, we explore the relationship between the size of the school district and both the number of elections needed to pass the budget and the size of the majority obtained on the passing election. Section V presents some evidence on the relationship of voter turnout and school district size. In Section VI we pose some simple tests of the effect of competition across jurisdictions on expenditure levels.

II. PERCEPTION AND INTERGOVERNMENTAL AID

In 1971-72, the year of our cross-sectional analysis, Oregon school districts received transfers from three higher levels of government. First and least (about 8 percent of spending statewide), there is federal aid; we have to ignore this since we have been unable to locate cross-sectional data on federal aid. Second, there is lump-sum state aid to districts in our cross-section. Third, there are payments from countywide Intermediate Education Districts (IEDs). State and IED payments each accounted for roughly one-fourth of total operating spending in the 111 districts in our cross-section.[4]

In Filimon, Romer, and Rosenthal (1982), we addressed the problem of fiscal illusion regarding intergovernmental aid payments. We developed a formal model--the "grant illusion" model--that includes perceptual parameters whose values are estimated from the data. A parametric specification that both captures perception effects and reflects legislated formulae is given by:

$$E^* = (1 - \rho)A + \max\ [(1 - \gamma)I,\ (B + V)] \quad \text{in 32 counties,}$$

$$E^* = (1 - \rho)A + (1 - \gamma)I + B + V \quad \text{in 4 counties,}$$

---

[3]Notable exceptions to this neglect are Enelow and Hinich (1980), McKelvey (1980), and Shepsle (1972).
[4]These are districts that both operate K-12 systems and appear on the school district census tape. For further details, see Romer and Rosenthal (forthcoming-b).

Voting and Spending

where

E^* = perceived expenditures per student
A = state aid per student
I = IED receipts per student
B = local expenditures "base" per student
V = amount (per student) in excess of base approved by voters.

When the perceptual parameters, ρ and γ, both equal zero, perceived expenditures equal actual expenditures, as determined by the above expressions which conform to state law and constitution. Similarly, the perceived reversion R^* is given by:[5,6]

$$R^* = (1 - \rho)A + \max[(1 - \gamma)I, B] \quad \text{in 32 counties,}$$

$$R^* = (1 - \rho)A + (1 - \gamma)I + B \quad \text{in 4 counties.}$$

In Filimon, Romer, and Rosenthal (1982), we used nonlinear maximum likelihood methods to estimate the model assuming full perception of the IED payments ($\gamma = 0$). Specifically, we estimated a log-linear model of the form:

$$\ln(E^*) = \beta_0 + \beta_1 \ln(Y^*) + \beta_2 \ln(P) + \beta_3 \ln(S) + \beta_4 H^*$$
$$+ \beta_5 \ln(Z^*) \qquad (1)$$

where

Y^* is an income term adjusted for perceived grants
P is tax price
S is students per household
$H^* = 1$ if $R^* \leq \mu$
$\quad = 0$ if $R^* > \mu$
μ is the reversion threshold to be estimated
$Z^* = \mu$ if $R^* \leq \mu$
$\quad = R^*$ if $R^* > \mu$.

[5] Only five of the 111 observations fall in the four counties with a special formula. These four counties, located in sparsely populated eastern Oregon, have traditionally been subject to special legislation.
[6] In the 32 county area, $B + V > I$ for all observations in the sample. Thus, for positive γ, E^* is not sensitive to variations in γ. However, since I is frequently greater than B, the perception of the IED payments is critical to the value of the reversion variables.

The model is linear in the β's but non-linear and discontinuous in the illusion parameter, ρ, and the threshold parameter, μ. The discontinuity was smoothed by the Tishler-Zang (1979) method.

Estimation of the $\gamma = 0$ model yielded a value for ρ of 0.97, indicating the presence of essentially complete fiscal illusion regarding state aid. To estimate perception of the IED payments, we initially held other parameters at the values that are maximum likelihood estimates for $\gamma = 0.0$ and then iterated over γ. To the fineness of the iteration, the likelihood is maximized for $\gamma = 0$. Moreover, the likelihood was greater when we used the complex, actual formula for the reversion in the 32 counties than when we assumed that voters acted as if the simpler, linear formula used in 4 eastern counties applied to the whole state. This result suggests that voters perceive the IED payments not in some *ad hoc*, heuristic fashion but in terms of the algebraic formula representing state law.

Non-linear estimation of the full model disclosed a global (for the computations) maximum at $\gamma = -0.54$. Comparison of likelihood values (see Table I) by the standard asymptotic test would clearly lead to rejection of the null hypothesis of $\gamma = 0.0$, suggesting that voters act as if IED aid were 50 percent greater than its actual amount.

Taking a cautious view of the asymptotic test, we would place more weight on the results obtained from maximizing the likelihood when γ is fixed, iterating from $\gamma = -1.0$ to $\gamma = 0.9$ by steps of 0.1. While the likelihood, as shown in Table I, oscillates over a relatively small range for negative γ, it is monotonically and sharply decreasing for positive γ. Furthermore, the estimates of ρ indicate strong misperception of state aid for all the values of γ, except for large positive ones where the likelihood is quite poor. Similarly, parameter estimates for the threshold and reversion effects (when they are identified) remain reasonably close to their $\gamma = 0.0$ values except for certain positive values of γ.[7]

---

[7]*The Tishler-Zang method smoothes the discontinuous function by using appropriate polynomials over a small interval $[-\delta, +\delta]$. Here $\delta = \$2$. The parameters μ, β_4, and β_5 are identified only when at least one observation lies in the interval. When parameters are reported as unidentified in Table I, the likelihood function was maximized at values where no observation was in the interval. Parameter estimates are quite insensitive to the choice of δ for $\delta \leq \$25$ until identification problems are encountered for small δ. Estimates were computed using the Berndt, Hall, Hall, and Hausman method in the MAXLIK program distributed by Bronwyn*

TABLE I. Parameter Estimates for Selected Values of γ^a

γ	Log-Likelihood	ρ	μ	β_4	β_5	Convergence
-1.0	-686	0.92	b	b	b	
-0.8	-680	0.81	256	0.21	0.22	c
-0.6	-677	0.82	b	b	b	
-0.54	-673	0.93	333	0.21	0.39	
-0.4	-682	0.88	b	b	b	
-0.2	-678	0.90	271	0.16	0.27	c
0.0	-683	0.97	211	0.15	0.18	
0.2	-692	0.98	278	-0.05	-0.10	
0.4	-695	1.01	b	b	b	
0.6	-700	0.78	278	0.40	0.54	
0.8	-723	0.78	158	0.05	0.09	c
0.9	-733	0.65	b	b	b	

^{a}For $\gamma = 0.00$, the values of the remaining parameters are $\beta_0 = -2.50$, $\beta_1 = 0.83$, $\beta_2 = -0.37$, $\beta_3 = -0.27$; for $\gamma = -0.54$, the values of the remaining parameters are $\beta_0 = -3.50$, $\beta_1 = 0.79$, $\beta_2 = -0.37$, $\beta_3 = -0.25$.
^{b}The parameter is not identified.
^{c}Convergence did not occur after 120 iterations.

We thus find that voters act as if there were no state aid, whereas IED monies are, if anything, exaggerated. This strong difference may be explained in terms of the information available to the voter. Whereas the IED is financed wholly by local property taxes which are known explicitly by homeowners, state aid is financed from general revenues. The voter can learn about state aid to his district only through deliberate inquiry or, possibly, through a chance media communication. Thus the linkage between taxation and spending is broken. We note that the agenda setters could convey the amount of state aid to the voters on the ballot but in practice uniformly elect not to do so. (This revealing piece of evidence comes from an interview with a school board lobbyist.) Both the omission of state aid amounts from the ballot and the results of the estimation of the perceptual expenditure model represent evidence at variance with the median

---

Hall Econometrics. For cost reasons, computation was stopped if the default convergence criterion was not met after 120 iterations. Substantial experience has shown that nearly all improvement in the likelihood function and changes in parameters take place in the first 20 iterations.

voter hypothesis. If elected officials sought to implement the demand of the median voter, they would seek to inform the voters of the true level of expenditure. Thus, the presence of fiscal illusion is incompatible with the median voter hypothesis.

A large number of more or less *ad hoc* regression studies (summarized in Gramlich, 1977) have indicated that the elasticities of lump-sum grants are greater than the elasticities of income. This "flypaper effect" is also incompatible with the proposition that competitive pressures force local officials to maximize the utility of some median voter.

III. BUDGET CUTS AND LEARNING

By restricting our attention to expenditures, we have neglected an important set of observations--the voting outcomes of budget elections. These outcomes can provide further tests of the setter model and enable us to improve our estimates of the expenditure equation. We developed an econometric specification that models expenditure and voting outcomes as a simultaneous process. This model incorporates the possibility that the setter has incomplete information regarding voter behavior. Voting is related to spending by an error components specification that characterizes the voting outcome as a function of the setter's error in the expenditure equation. In particular, the fraction of voters who vote Yes on a proposal is, under the setter model, hypothesized to be decreasing in the magnitude of the error the setter makes in the expenditure proposal. Preliminary results from this model are presented in Romer and Rosenthal (forthcoming-a). Simultaneous estimation of voting and expenditure does not significantly affect the estimates of the coefficients of the expenditure equation. The estimated voting equation is consistent with the hypotheses of the setter model.

Rather than elaborate on these single-election outcomes, we would like to present here some results from voting in sequences of elections. When a budget election fails, the school board may try again (up to six or eight times in a school year, depending on current state law). An interesting question is whether setters can learn from their errors in a sequence of elections. Budget cuts may not in themselves be evidence of learning. When a setter has complete knowledge of voter preferences but faces random turnout, Romer and Rosenthal (1979) show that a setter maximizing the expected budget optimally chooses a sequence of decreasing budget proposals. Since preferences are known in this situation, any particular stochastic realization in an election provides no new information, and the setter would not be led to modify his sequence of proposals. Romer and Rosenthal (1979) present evidence from Oregon, covering all districts from 1970-71 through 1976-77, showing that proposal increases are rare and that most districts exhibit cuts between elections although many districts maintain their initial proposal.

This pattern is borne out for our sample of 111 districts in 1971-72. There were 41 districts where the first proposal was defeated. Of these, twenty-eight districts cut their proposals from the first election to the winning election, while eleven had "no change." Only two districts showed proposal increases over the sequence.

In contrast to the full-information case, if the setter has incomplete information on preferences, the election outcomes can result in learning. Assume that the districts are identical in the information available to the setter (e.g., the per student reversion) but distinct in other ways (e.g., actual preferences). A strong negative vote would suggest cutting the budget more than would a negative vote close to 50 percent. In fact, a vote close to 50 percent might lead to an increased proposal on a later ballot. Because he has more than one try, a budget-maximizing setter might well make an initial proposal where the expected vote percentage was less than 50 (see Romer and Rosenthal, 1979). A percentage closer to 50 than the expected percentage would indicate higher spending preferences than expected, leading to an increased proposal on a subsequent ballot.

Thus, learning combined with uncertainty would suggest increases as well as cuts, although the eleven "no change" observations in our 1971-72 sample suggest the presence of considerations of year-to-year strategy or unwillingness to do "fine tuning," factors that are not part of our current discussion. We should, however, expect to find a negative relationship between the first election vote and the spending cut; that is, the difference between the initial proposal and the final proposal. Our 1971-72 sample provides preliminary support for such a relationship. For descriptive purposes only, we computed the squared linear correlation between the vote logit[8] and the difference between the first proposal and the final proposal. That squared correlation is .215 with a t-statistic of -3.27 (p = .0011). While examination of a scatter plot disclosed a far from linear relationship, it also supported the finding of a negative relationship. In

[8] *The vote logit is ln(% Yes Vote/% No Vote).*

fact all seven districts that had very poor election results, with over 60 percent No votes, cut their budget proposals. Setters do indeed appear to learn from their errors.[9]

Of course, the districts in our sample are not identical with respect to setter information. Our suggestive results must thus be confirmed by more sophisticated tests.

IV. THE SIZE OF MAJORITIES

The size of majorities in losing budget referenda was seen to explain some of the variance of subsequent budget cuts, supporting the prediction of a setter model with learning. We now examine the size of majorities in both winning and losing elections to provide a direct comparison of the setter and median voter models. This comparison does not require the use of any census data, so we are able to present data for more than 300 school districts over the seven year period, 1970-76.

In making this comparison, we assume that a citizen who votes against a proposal does so if and only if he prefers the reversion to the proposal. Under certain turnout and full information about preferences, a setter intent on maximizing the utility of the median voter would propose this voter's ideal point. This proposal would always win. Moreover, if the reversion is less than the median ideal point, majorities substantially larger than 50 percent should occur. To see this, note that the median voter and all voters who desire expenditures larger than the median will vote for the proposal when the proposal is the median ideal point. In addition, many of those whose ideal points are below the median will support the proposal. For example, if induced preferences over expenditures are symmetric about the ideal point, all citizens with ideal points greater than halfway between the reversion and the median will support the proposal. Since many of our observations have very low reversions (40 of the sample of 111 in the 1971-72 expenditure regressions fell below the threshold), one could expect many very large majorities. Under uncertainty, one would expect to find some losing proposals, but the average majority should continue to be distinctly larger than 50 percent.

In contrast, the setter model under certainty would predict exactly 50 percent (plus one vote) in all cases. The

---

[9] The original version of this paper, available from the authors, contains graphs that provide more information on these results (see Romer and Rosenthal, 1981).

Voting and Spending

uncertainty predictions are less clear (see Romer and Rosenthal, 1979), but one might expect to find outcomes clustered about 50 percent in a reasonably symmetric fashion.

To see how voting outcomes vary with the size of the school district, we regressed the proportion voting No in the first election of a school year on the logarithm of the district's enrollment. (We also controlled for the type of school district.) The results of these regressions, for the years 1970 through 1976, are reported in Table II. Clearly, the proportion voting No increases with district size. Using .04 as the value of the coefficient of the enrollment variable, one would estimate that if a district with 100 students were to vote 48% No, one with 5000 students would vote 52% No.

A detailed look at the data discloses strong empirical regularities repeated from one year to the next.[10] First, very small districts (those with fewer than 100 voters) do appear consistent with the median voter model. Proposals in those districts almost always pass, and they pass with large margins, often in excess of a 75 percent majority. In some tiny districts, there are unanimously approved proposals. Second, as district size increases, the large majorities vanish. This result is clearly at odds with a certainty median voter model. Can the result be reconciled with median voter politics by arguing the setter has poor information as to the median voter's ideal point in the large districts? We think not.

What a median voter oriented politican would propose under uncertainty is unclear. The politician cannot readily exploit a sequence of elections to pinpoint the median voter because (1) only a small number of elections is available and

---

[10]*An interesting way to exhibit voting patterns is to consider the variable $P = ln[(EL/2) + NO]$ where EL is the number of the passing election (EL = 1, 2, 3...) and NO is the ratio of No votes to total voting in the passing election. Thus, P is a lexicographic index of conflict between the setter and the electorate. The greater the number of elections needed to pass a budget, the more the conflict. For a given election number, conflict is increasing in the No vote. In figures that were deleted from the final version of this paper, we plotted P against the logarithm of district size, measured as total voting in the first election. (This measure of size correlates very highly with enrollment. The analysis has also been replicated with enrollment as the measure of size, with parallel results.) Our verbal summary in the text is based on these figures, which are in Romer and Rosenthal (1981).*

TABLE II. Voting, Size, and School System Type
Dependent Variable: Proportion Voting No, First Election

Coefficient	1970	1971	1972	1973	1974	1975	1976
Constant	.136[c]	.118[d]	.109[c]	.148[d]	.167[d]	.159[d]	.228[d]
	(.037)	(.034)	(.033)	(.034)	(.035)	(.035)	(.035)
Ln(ADM)	.050[d]	.049[d]	.046[d]	.044[d]	.038[d]	.043[d]	.037[d]
(Enrollment)	(.005)	(.005)	(.005)	(.005)	(.005)	(.005)	(.005)
Union High[a]	.008	.013	.042	-.015	.025	.082[c]	.039
	(.026)	(.025)	(.025)	(.025)	(.025)	(.025)	(.025)
Unified Elem.[a]	-.045	-.059[c]	-.094[c]	-.090[c]	-.058	-0.84[c]	-.079[c]
	(.032)	(0.29)	(.029)	(.030)	(.030)	(.030)	(.030)
Elementary[a]	.002	.012	-.002	.036[c]	.003	.025	-.002
	(.018)	(.017)	(.016)	(.017)	(.016)	(.016)	(.016)
R^2	.35	.37	.42	.42	.29	.38	.32
N	324	324	316	318	314	312	305
Mean Proportion Voting No	0.42	0.40	0.37	0.38	0.38	0.42	0.44
Max. Proportion Voting No[b]	0.76	0.77	0.71	0.72	0.75	0.74	0.72

[a] These are 0-1 dummy variables. The school district types subsumed in the constant are K-12 (Unified and Unified A) districts.
[b] The minimum of the Proportion Voting No was zero in each of the years listed.
[c] The coefficient is more than twice the standard error (standard errors in parentheses).
[d] The coefficient is more than four times the standard error (standard errors in parentheses).

(2) the sequence must stop once a majority votes Yes. Consequently, proposals would depend, in a complex fashion on the reversion and expectations concerning the entire utility function of at least the median voter.

In spite of the complexities introduced by uncertainty, it is nonetheless interesting to assume that there is at most only a small bias of proposals about median ideal points. This assumption leads to two empirical predictions for the median voter model. First, we would still expect to see the proposal win more than half the time. But in large districts (those with more than 1000 voters) the first election ends in defeat about as often as it ends in victory. Second, at least occasionally, the lack of information should lead to a proposal below the median. In this case, the majority voting Yes should be greater than in the certainty case. So, if the setter has poorer information in large districts than in smaller districts and if the spread of preferences is similar in large and small districts, we should expect to see some majorities in large districts that are larger than those in small districts. We do not observe this. Big wins occur almost exclusively in small districts. For example, first election majorities in excess of 75 percent almost never occur in districts with more than 300 voters although such majorities are numerous in smaller districts. Furthermore, when a second election is required, large majorities continue to tend to occur only in small districts.

In contrast, the large district outcomes are certainly not inconsistent with the setter model.[11] The setter model could be supported even in the small districts by a claim that the large majorities there result from a greater homogeneity of preferences in smaller districts. But any claim of homogeneity for small districts requires further evidence. We explored various statistics of the income distribution (decile ratios, etc.) for the census based sample of 11 districts that were in our expenditure regressions. We failed to uncover any evidence supporting a claim of less income variation in smaller districts. Of course, even the smallest of these 111 districts is relatively large compared to the districts that have very large majorities. Moreover, income dispersion is only one possible measure of heterogeneity. Still, a conservative treatment of the issue would award the small districts to the median voter school in the absence of further evidence.

[11]*Fortunately, the districts we previously used in the expenditure regressions are all among the larger districts, since the census tape was restricted to districts with enrollments over 250 (corresponding to roughly 125 voters).*

To summarize these results, it seems that median voter democracy appears to prosper only in a pristine world of very small communities. When school districts attain a size of roughly 2000 students, which is large only by Oregon standards, Niskanen's budget-maximizer apparently makes his entrance. It is not surprising that the school lobby has so vigorously pushed for consolidations.

V. VOTER TURNOUT IN BUDGET ELECTIONS

If median voter outcomes hold in small districts and budget-maximizing occurs in large districts, a reasonable conjecture is that citizen participation in elections is greater in smaller districts.[12] We do not have reliable data on voter registration by school district, and population figures are available only for the census year. To measure voter turnout, we divided total voting by the district's enrollment. Table III shows that turnout does indeed decline with district size. Also, the interest generated by the failure of a budget election leads to greater turnout. For example, a district passing its budget on the third try gen-

---

[12]*See Tullock (1968) and Riker and Ordeshook (1968). In the Riker-Ordeshook model, turnout depends on the product of the subjective probability (p) of casting a decisive vote and the utility difference (b) of two alternatives.* Ceteris paribus, *the probability of casting a decisive vote declines with the size of the electorate. While the higher turnouts observed in national elections in comparison to local ones seems to go counter to this model, it should be recalled that b is not held constant between national and local arenas. In contrast, for school elections, b, as it relates to per student spending, will be roughly independent of jurisdiction size. Variations in turnout would therefore be due to variations in p.*

In one way, however, our regression model is probably biased against finding a significant size effect. The p term depends not only on size but also on a subjective estimate of how close the outcome is to a 50-50 split. [Witness the historically low turnout in Presidential elections in the American South; see also Rosenthal and Sen (1973).] Since we know from the previous section that referenda are usually not close in small districts, the size effect should be even larger were we able to control for prior expectations about the outcome.

TABLE III. Determinants of Turnout--Winning Election[a]
Dependent Variable: Ln(Total Voting/Enrollment)

Coefficient	1970	1971	1972	1973	1974	1975	1976
Constant	1.605[c]	1.168[c]	1.551[c]	2.529[c]	2.256[c]	2.064[c]	1.788[c]
	(0.230)	(0.221)	(0.232)	(0.526)	(0.405)	(0.239)	(0.242)
Ln (ADM)	-0.236[c]	-0.212[c]	-0.231[c]	-0.285[c]	-0.258[c]	-0.235[c]	-0.232[c]
(Enrollment)	(0.023)	(0.020)	(0.021)	(0.021)	(0.022)	(0.022)	(0.025)
Union High[b]	0.510[c]	0.539[c]	0.635[c]	0.572[c]	0.640[c]	0.652[c]	0.690[c]
	(0.113)	(0.099)	(0.107)	(0.111)	(0.115)	(0.116)	(0.121)
Unified Elem.[b]	0.057	0.217	0.146	0.166	0.189	0.283[c]	0.292[c]
	(0.136)	(0.116)	(0.125)	(0.129)	(0.136)	(0.129)	(0.146)
Elementary[b]	-0.032	0.016	0.034	-0.002	0.044	0.120	0.158
	(0.076)	(0.066)	(0.071)	(0.072)	(0.075)	(0.074)	(0.083)
Budget Passed in 1st Election[b]	-0.723[c]	-0.437[c]	-0.629[c]	-1.378[c]	-1.181[c]	-1.068[c]	-0.667[c]
	(0.162)	(0.168)	(0.176)	(0.497)	(0.309)	(0.172)	(0.168)
Budget Passed in 2nd Election[b]	-0.500[c]	-0.152	-0.410[c]	-1.138[c]	-0.934[c]	-0.987[c]	-0.541[c]
	(0.167)	(0.176)	(0.194)	(0.499)	(0.375)	(0.179)	(0.178)
Budget Passed in 3rd Election[b]	-0.440[c]	-0.323	-0.281	-1.089[c]	-0.787[c]	-0.633[c]	-0.229
	(0.182)	(0.186)	(0.200)	(0.509)	(0.386)	(0.194)	(0.189)
R^2	.36	.43	.44	.51	.46	.48	.45
N	324	324	316	318	314	312	305

[a]Districts with ADM = 0 in voting year or districts with no election were deleted from the sample.
[b]These are 0-1 dummy variables. K-12 districts and proposals passing on fourth election or later are subsumed in the constant.
[c]The coefficient is more than twice the standard error (standard errors in parentheses).

erates as much as a 33 percent higher turnout in the winning election, *ceteris paribus*, than a district whose budget passes on the first ballot.

VI. SMSA VS. OTHER DISTRICTS

Voter mobility among jurisdictions is generally viewed as a force that constrains the monopoly power of suppliers of local public goods.[13] Competition among jurisdictions is likely to be greatest within metropolitan areas, where inter-jurisdictional moves are relatively inexpensive and can typically be accomplished without changing jobs. In more isolated areas, this kind of shopping among alternative locations is much more costly. To the extent that such mobility-induced competition exists, it would tend to reduce the setter's power in metropolitan districts relative to more isolated districts. Consequently, the estimated expenditure equation based on the setter model might be a poorer predictor in the former types in districts.

Using our estimate of equation (1) for 1971-72, we examined the residuals for districts in five counties that lie in SMSAs (Portland, Salem, and Eugene metropolitan areas). A crude hypothesis would be that residuals in SMSAs would be negative because of competition among districts. Table IV summarizes our findings. The county spending residuals in SMSAs appear similar to those found statewide.

We also estimated (for 1976-77 only) voting and turnout regressions like those in Tables II and III, including dummy variables for SMSA counties. None of these variables had coefficients significantly different from zero. If there is any systematic difference in spending and voting between districts in metropolitan areas and those outside these areas, more refined distinctions need to be made than are captured by our admittedly rough-and-ready tests.

VII. CONCLUSION

Over the past several years, we have developed and tested a model of the local public finance process in the institutional setting of referenda. We posited that the

---

[13]*Epple and Zelenitz (1981) show that citizen mobility alone does not eliminate a public good supplier's monopoly power when jurisdictional boundaries are fixed.*

TABLE IV. Expenditure Residuals in SMSA Counties

County	Average Residual	Std. Dev. of Residual[a]	Root Mean Squared Residual[b]	N
Lane	0.117	0.122	0.166	15
Clackamas	-0.005	0.194	0.173	5
Multnomah	0.005	0.083	0.059	4
Washington	0.031	0.142	0.134	6
Marion	-0.109	0.124	0.157	6
Total Sample	0.000	0.167	0.162	111

[a] The standard deviation for each county (taken about county mean residual) was computed with division by $N-1$. The statewide sample standard deviation was computed with division by $N-6$.

[b] Root mean squared errors (taken about zero) were computed with division by N.

agenda would be controlled by setters seeking to maximize the expected budget. This paper has provided additional empirical support for the setter model.

Earlier findings, reviewed in Section I, revealed that the reversion significantly affects actual spending. We have now also found suggestive evidence (Section III) that, when an initial referendum fails, the difference between actual spending and the initial proposal is consistent with learning by a budget-maximizing setter.

Can agenda control by the setter persist as a political equilibrium? There are two ways in which agenda control might be upset. First, voters could vote with their feet, inducing interjurisdictional competition among setters. Second, voters could, in the election of candidates for office, promote intrajurisdictional competition for control of the agenda.

As to the first mode of competition, it does not appear to be critical in Oregon. At least, the analysis of SMSA residuals in Section VI suggested our results are robust to the possible presence of interjurisdictional effects.

As to the second possibility, intrajurisdictional competition will be effective only when voters are politically active and informed. The costs of information and participation are unlikely to be strongly dependent on jurisdictional size, but the impact of personal participation and voting declines with the size of the electorate. Judging from our results on turnout (Section V) as well as from the size of majorities (Section IV), the cost of developing more moderate proposals is sufficiently high that agenda control is likely to persist in all but the smallest jurisdictions.

In any event, we emphasize that, even in the case of single-peaked preferences, the median preference will in general be enacted only under highly special conditions that include, in addition to open agendas or platforms, binary voting by fully informed voters.

Consistent with the interests of budget-maximizers, the institutional process of school finance is remote from these conditions. School boards are not a single executive but an unpaid committee elected for staggered terms. Information about state aid in the local budget appears to be effectively masked from the electorate, a result that is robust to our inclusion of the more readily apparent IED payments (Section II).

The evidence, then, argues for continued interest in agenda control models. Yet the setter model, as well as the standard median voter model, is purely static. Dynamic elements make the picture more complex and the range of potential outcomes richer. We would venture that the dynamic path is one of fairly discontinuous adjustments, reflecting rapid changes in information and political organization, rather than one of fine tuning about some quite stable median position. Indeed, the presence and apparent success of political entrepreneurs such as Howard Jarvis and Ronald Reagan suggest that spending excesses can go only "so far." The response to these reactions against "big" government, together with the study of the extent to which such reactions do indeed attain their stated goals, provides an important and fascinating set of problems for theoretical and empirical research.

REFERENCES

Enelow, J., and M. J. Hinich, 1980. "A New Approach to Voter Uncertainty in the Downsian Spatial Model," *American Journal of Political Science* 25:483-493.

Epple, D., and A. Zelenitz, 1981. "The Implications of Competition among Jurisdictions: Does Tiebout Need Politics?", *Journal of Political Economy* 89:1197-1217.

Filimon, R., T. Romer, and H. Rosenthal, 1982. "Asymmetric Information and Agenda Control: The Bases of Monopoly Power in Public Spending," *Journal of Public Economics* 17:51-70.

Gramlich, E. M., 1977. "Intergovernmental Grants: A Review of the Empirical Literature," in *The Political Economy of Fiscal Federalism*, W. E. Oates (ed.). Lexington, Mass.: D. C. Heath.

McKelvey, R. D., 1980. "Ambiguity in Spatial Models of Policy Formation," *Public Choice* 35:385-402.

Niskanen, W. A., 1971. *Bureaucracy and Representative Government*. Chicago: Aldine.

Riker, W. H., and P. C. Ordeshook, 1968. "A Theory of the Calculus of Voting," *American Political Science Review* 62:25-42.

Romer, T., and H. Rosenthal, 1978. "Political Resource Allocation, Controlled Agendas, and the Status Quo," *Public Choice* 33: 27-43.

Romer, T., and H. Rosenthal, 1979. "Bureaucrats vs. Voters: On the Political Economy of Resource Allocation by Direct Democracy," *Quarterly Journal of Economics* 93:563-587.

Romer, T., and H. Rosenthal, 1980. "An Institutional Theory of the Effect of Intergovernmental Grants," *National Tax Journal* 33:451-458.

Romer, T., and H. Rosenthal, 1981. "Voting and Spending," GSIA Working Paper, Carnegie-Mellon University.

Romer, T., and H. Rosenthal, forthcoming-a. "An Exploration in the Politics and Economics of Local Public Services," *Zeitschrift fur Nationalokonomie/Journal of Economics*.

Romer, T., and H. Rosenthal, forthcoming-b. "Median Voters or Budget Maximizers: Evidence from School Expenditure Referenda," *Economic Inquiry*.

Rosenthal, H., and S. Sen, 1973. "Electoral Participation in the French Fifth Republic," *American Political Science Review* 67:29-54.

Shepsle, K. A., 1972. "The Strategy of Ambiguity, Uncertainty and Electoral Competition," *American Political Science Review* 66:555-568.

Tishler, A., and I. Zang, 1979. "A Switching Regression Method Using Inequality Conditions," *Journal of Econometrics* 11:259-274.

Tullock, G., 1968. *Towards a Mathematics of Politics*. Ann Arbor, Mich.: University of Michigan Press.